ESSENTIAL GEAR

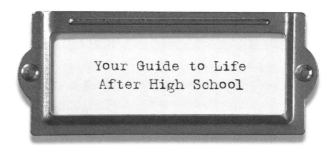

Your Guide to Life
After High School

D1521530

LifeWay Press®
Nashville, Tennessee

ISBN: 1-4158-2805-9
Item Number: 001274582

Dewey Decimal Classification Number: 248.83
Subject Heading: CHRISTIAN LIFE \ HIGH SCHOOL GRADUATES

Printed in the United States of America

Student Ministry Publishing
LifeWay Church Resources
One LifeWay Plaza
Nashville, Tennessee 37234-0174

We believe the Bible has God for its author; salvation for its end; and truth, without any
mixture of error, for its matter and that all Scripture is totally true and trustworthy. The 2000
statement of *The Baptist Faith and Message* is our doctrinal guideline.

CONTENTS

WRITERS

BILL BANKS has more than 20 years of youth and college ministry experience. He has led mission projects in five states and two foreign countries. Bill and his wife, Brenda, have two daughters, Angela and Allison. Bill is the minister of education and students at Western Hills Baptist Church in Wichita Falls, Texas.

KELLY KING is the women's ministry coordinator/communications director for Council Road Baptist Church in Bethany, Oklahoma. She has a degree in journalism from Oklahoma Baptist University. Kelly and her husband, Vic, have two children, Conner and Courtney.

BUBBA RAINWATER is a college and singles minister at Burnt Hickory Baptist Church in Marietta, Georgia. He and his wife, Ashlie, have a daughter, Holland, and twin boys, Cort and Caden. He enjoys writing and playing beach volleyball.

CASEY ROSS is the family pastor at Edwards Road Baptist Church in Greenville, South Carolina. He has degrees from Presbyterian College and The Southern Baptist Theological Seminary. He and his wife, Julie, love playing with their 3-year-old daughter, Bennett. Casey also enjoys reading, watching and playing sports, and writing.

DIANNE WADE grew up as a military child in Virginia and Maryland. Eventually her family settled in Mississippi until her high school graduation. She attended colleges in Mississippi and Louisiana where she majored in art education and elementary education. She holds a master's degree in curriculum and instruction. She now teaches elementary and high school art. She and her husband, Bill, have two children—Katy and Joey.

Imagine you are about to take your first bungee jump—not a little bungee jump at an amusement park, but a jump from a high bridge over a gaping canyon. Also suppose the equipment expert who is helping you get rigged up is called away, and another person is called in to finish harnessing you. Looking down at the canyon floor below, you wonder—*Did the two guys cover all the bases? Or did they miss something between the two of them?* What are the odds you would have ignored the help of the second guy and just jumped off the bridge with your rigging and harness half-complete?

Without a doubt, leaving adolescence for young adulthood is a bungee jump. Some make the jump fine and adjust well into adult life. Some crash on the ground below because they were unprepared. In our analogy, the first equipment expert represents the caring and competent youth leaders in your church. They've been doing everything possible to prepare you for life after high school, to strengthen your relationship with God. However, they always run out of time before they can finish the job. They leave you standing on the bridge with your rigging incomplete. You still need further preparation—preparation that comes from a growing relationship with God beyond high school. Ignoring that relationship in your young adult years guarantees that some of your gear is incomplete—a disaster waiting to happen.

When you graduate from high school, you don't graduate from your relationship with God or other believers. Just as you are becoming more mature physically, emotionally, and socially, you can become more mature spiritually as well. The pages of this book and the materials on the CD-ROM are designed to help you on that journey to greater maturity. Use this resource as a reference guide when you need it. Refer to it when you struggle with changing relationships, finances, purpose, or work. Allow the truths to help further prepare you for that bungee jump into adult life. Strap in and hang on for the ride of your life.

Success in life is a matter not so much of talent or opportunity as of concentration and perseverance.
—C.W. Wendte

Chapter 1

STAYING STRONG

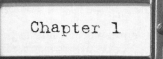

Where's the first aid kit? Are you feeling OK? Do you hurt anywhere? Do you realize there is an epidemic going around? This particular epidemic has common symptoms for a select group of people in all areas of America. It affects males and females alike and occurs in the late fall to spring. Thankfully it isn't fatal, but it is often quite contagious. There are no shots or pills to prevent or minimize its effects. Your teachers dread it, your parents fear it, and you are highly susceptible to it. Chances are pretty good that you are experiencing symptoms of this disease or possibly have already developed a full-blown case. What is it? Senioritis.

"Senioritis," or "senior slump," affects a large portion of about 3 million senior students nationwide.[1] How do you know if you have it or are catching it? What are the symptoms?

Teachers see this malady as a lack of interest and a general slacking off in attitude, grades, and attendance. Parents often see it as laziness and disrespect, and they fear that it may become a permanent problem. Teens, however, see it in a different light.

The senior year brings about a series of events that will forever change the way you see yourself, your family, your friends, your faith, and the future. This definitely can create some insecurities and fears. It is also the beginning of many lasts—the last pep rally, the last football game, the last formal dance, and the last credits before graduation.

Senioritis! How Did I Get This?

The causes of senioritis can be as varied as the students. Examine the table for some facts about senioritis.

Cause	Effect	Result
Colleges often base a student's acceptance on grades after the first semester of the senior year.	Students see little need in keeping up their grades and usual course work once accepted into a college.	Colleges are catching on and starting to check grades and courses after the second semester. Some reserve the right to rescind the admissions acceptance if grades drop too much or if a student takes lower-level classes.[2] As many as 30 percent of entering college freshmen require remedial course work.[3]
Seniors have a lot on their minds— social life, family, graduation, jobs, money, college preparation.	Students experience a lack of sleep and spend less time on school-work.	Grades drop and atten-dance becomes optional. Inattention to schoolwork can result in not earning credits or not attending the required days to meet graduation requirements.
Some seniors feel they deserve a year off. They have worked hard for three years and want a break.	This attitude becomes a lifestyle and carries over into college.	The largest percentage of students to drop out of college are freshmen.[4]

Self-Diagnosis

Senioritis may seem unavoidable; however, many students actually manage to avoid a serious case, and a few avoid it altogether. Before moving on and assuming you have been bitten by this bug, check yourself out.

Look at the list of symptoms on the next page and check the frequency you are experiencing them.

Symptom	Never	Sometimes	Usually
Sleeping late and missing early classes			
Failing to complete homework assignments or study for tests			
Putting less effort into projects and papers			
Cutting classes			
Sleeping or daydreaming frequently in class			
Finding shortcuts, sometimes unethically, to complete assignments			
Losing interest in high school events			
Choosing classes that are less challenging			
Challenging parents, teachers, or employers about issues—important or not			
Waking up dreading going to school			

Diagnosis

If you checked "never" most often: You are good to go!

If you checked "sometimes" most often: You've been exposed, but there's still a chance to get over it.

If you checked "usually" most often: Get help right away!

Further Diagnosis

Results may still be inconclusive. Check the statements that have gone through your mind recently to examine the extent you've been affected by this bug.

- [ ] **I've worked hard for three years, and now it's time to have fun.**
- [ ] **Next year will be tough, with real adult expectations, so I'm taking a break this year.**
- [ ] **There are admissions forms to complete, entrance essays to write, colleges to visit. I don't have time for high school like I did last year.**

- ☐ I'm not going to college, so my senior year doesn't really matter. I just want to graduate.
- ☐ I've goofed off for the last three years. Why should this year be any different?
- ☐ The military already has my name on the dotted line. My senior grades won't affect that.
- ☐ I don't plan on getting a job. Why bother?
- ☐ The senior year is all about being with friends, hanging out, and making memories. School is just a necessity.
- ☐ I'll work hard until I get an acceptance letter or promise of a job. Then it's sliding into home for me.

Checking any of these statements is cause for concern. Were you surprised to find that you already have some symptoms of "slumping"?

The senior year brings about a series of events that will forever change the way you see yourself, your family, your friends, your faith, and the future.

Dealing with Senioritis

Being a Christian does not give you immunity to senioritis, but it can change the way you deal with it. As a Christian teen experiencing the long-awaited senior year, how much senioritis is OK? Where should you draw the line? Take a look at two people in the Bible and see how different things might have been had they given in to an ancient strain of senioritis.

Joseph Never Gave Up

Remember Joseph, Jacob's son? He was an intelligent, good-looking young man, about 17 or 18, when his brothers sold him into slavery. (See Gen. 37; 39.) This would be a great excuse to give up. But Joseph chose to make the best of this situation. His owner, Potiphar, was so impressed with his work ethic that "he did not concern himself with anything except the food he ate" (Gen. 39:6). Potiphar's wife, however, was impressed with Joseph's appearance. She accused Joseph falsely, and he landed in prison. (See Gen. 39:6-20.) Now he *really* had a reason to quit.

The decisions he made as a teen and young man eventually changed the course of history for the Jews.

Instead, Joseph used every available opportunity to show that the Lord was with him. He became the warden's assistant and did such a good job that "the warden did not bother with anything under Joseph's authority" (Gen. 39:23). There is more to Joseph's story as he matured into an adult, but the decisions he made as a teen and young man eventually changed the course of history for the Jews (Hebrews) and set up a historical chain of events that led to the birth of Christ.

Esther: For Such a Time as This

Esther was a young Hebrew girl, probably a teen, living in captivity in a foreign country when she caught the king's eye. She and many other girls were specifically chosen to spend a year preparing themselves in hopes of being chosen as the next queen. This included daily beauty treatments and special food. She also had seven maids to meet her every need. (See Esth. 2:8-9.) This was pretty nice treatment, but it meant she would be separated from her friends and family. She realized that even after all of this preparation she might not be chosen. But Esther continued to prepare for her future and eventually was chosen as the queen. She was placed in a position to save her people, the Jews, from annihilation. (See Esth. 8:5-6.) Imagine the fate of the Jews if Esther had declined the king's offer and had chosen to stay in captivity with her friends because she didn't want the hassle.

Imagine the fate of the Jews if Esther had declined the king's offer and had chosen to stay in captivity with her friends because she didn't want the hassle.

Joseph and Esther both chose to fulfill their purposes rather than slack off and take it easy. How do their examples fit into your life as a senior? It isn't as big a stretch as you might think. They didn't have the same expectations you might be experiencing, such as college or career choices, car and insurance payments, and busy social lives; but they did have something in common: they each had a commitment to God.

Is It Really Such a Bad Thing?

Could it be that senioritis is not just a phase that seniors must go through, like a rite of passage, but rather a chosen, deliberate behavior? If it is a choice, do your choices please God and bring honor to Him?

The Apostle Paul (follower of Jesus who wrote over half of the New Testament) would respond to seniors wanting to ease off their senior year by saying something like, "Whatever you do, do it enthusiastically, as something done for the Lord and not for men, knowing that you will receive the reward of an inheritance from the Lord—you serve the Lord Christ" (Col. 3:23-24). Ouch! Does that hurt just a little? The "whatevers" include your senior year and all that goes with it.

While you may not think your life makes a difference like Paul's did, you'd really be amazed at the impact you have on others. People are looking at your life.

How enthusiastically did you complete your last English or science project? Were you enthusiastic about the classes you chose to take? Have you been filling out college or job applications as for the Lord? OK, that does sound a bit weird, but what does it mean to do something as for the Lord? You don't yet know all the specific plans He has for you. However, being at college, at a specific job, or entering the military is part of the overall plan for your life. It could be one of the BIG parts.

What was Paul teaching Timothy in 2 Timothy 4:5? Insert your name for the word *you*. "But as for (you) _____, keep a clear head about everything, endure hardship, do the work of an evangelist, fulfill your ministry."

Paul lived his life as an example that Timothy could follow. Paul's whole purpose in life was to bring others to Christ. His constant examples of faith, patience, love, and endurance pointed others to Christ. While you may not think your life makes a difference like Paul's did, you'd really be amazed at the impact you have on others. People are looking at your life.

Gear Up to Win

The senior year is tough and challenging. It is a true test of endurance and character. It takes about 180 days to complete, and the reward at the end is more than a diploma, a tassel, and the privilege of being out of school. Each person runs the race in a different style and with different equipment. Choosing how to pace yourself and developing strategies to help you finish can often seem like too much for one person to bear.

Paul wrote the ultimate encouragement in Hebrews 12:1-2: "Therefore since we also have such a large cloud of witnesses surrounding us, let us lay aside every weight and the sin that so easily ensnares us, and run with endurance the race that lies before us, keeping our eyes on Jesus, the source and perfecter of our faith." However, you are not alone in your struggle. You are not running this senior race alone. You have a cheering squad surrounding you. Those who have gone before you are calling your name and urging you toward the finish line, encouraging you to keep your eyes on Jesus each step of the way. They have already run the race and know the rewards. And it was worth it.

Extra Credit

- In the back of this book is a CD-ROM. Pop it into your computer and go to the section "The Senior Year and Beyond." Print out "Finishing Strong." Take time to memorize these verses.
- Write on a card Paul's words of encouragement to the Ephesians and put it in a place where you can see it every day and memorize it: "Finally, be strengthened by the Lord and by His vast strength" (Eph. 6:10).
- Develop an accountability group among the seniors in your youth group. Hold each other accountable for doing your best throughout the year. Meet at school during the week to encourage one another.

1. Mekeisha Madden, "Tuned-out kids risk graduation, college," *Detroit News* [online], 17 March 2004 [cited 15 Oct 2004]. Available from Internet: *www.detnews.com.*
2. "What to Do about 'Senioritis'," CollegeBoard.com [online], 2004, [cited 15 Oct 2004]. Available from Internet: *www.collegeboard.com.*
3. Demaree K. Michelau, "What's the Cure for Senioritis?" State Legislatures [online] June 2002 [cited 15 Oct 2004]. Available from Internet: *www.ncsl.org.*
4. Dave Newbart, " 'Senioritis' can be lethal to students," *Chicago Sun-Times* [online], 1 Aug 2004 [cited 15 Oct 2004]. Available from Internet: *www.suntimes.com.*

Truth is the heart of morality.
—Thomas Huxley

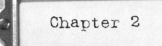

Chapter 2

NOTHING BUT THE TRUTH

15

What is truth? Throw out things like urban legends and endless arguments over sports and fashions and think for a moment. Ask yourself the question, *What is truth?* Then try to answer that question. It's tough, isn't it? In the Gospel of John, an amazing encounter took place between the Roman governor of Palestine, Pontius Pilate, and Jesus of Nazareth. Pilate took Jesus to a back room to ask Him a few questions. What began with direct questions about the accusations made by the Jewish leaders ended with Pilate asking the ultimate question: "What is truth?" (John 18:38).

Why does it matter if we know truth or not? Because truth provides purpose—a foundation upon which to build our lives.

More Than True Statements

When Pilate asked Jesus about truth, he wasn't asking Jesus to tell him true things; he was asking Jesus to tell him the greater truths of life. In other words, Pilate didn't want to know if the sky was blue or if an apple was red. Pilate wanted to know about right and wrong, just and unjust, wisdom and foolishness. He wanted to know what we all, on some level, really want to know—what is true and what is false? What do we base our lives on? What is our guide for living?

Someone once defined *truth* as "reality as known by the one for whom reality can be known in all its completeness." Yeah, that's a deep concept, so let's see if we can simplify that definition a bit. The good ol' *Merriam Webster's Collegiate® Dictionary, Tenth Edition* defines *truth* as "the body of real things, events, or facts: actuality." In other words, truth corresponds to reality. And that reality can only be fully known by someone or something that can actually know everything. Truth can only fully be known by someone or something that has the capacity to know and comprehend all truth. Human beings can know bits and pieces of truth, but you and I cannot know all truth. So who can know all truth? God.

16 The Only One Who Knows

The Bible clearly states that God is eternal—He had no beginning, and He has no end. Have you ever thought about the fact that God existed long before He created this universe? It is hard to comprehend, but God knows the complete history of everything from beginning to end because He lives outside the scope of time. The story of humanity and this world may have begun on the first day of creation, but God did not. He has always existed, and He always will. In Revelation 22:13 Jesus described Himself as the "Alpha and Omega," or the beginning and the end. Because God is timeless, He alone can fully understand everything in time.

But is God omniscient (a fancy word for "all-knowing")? Does God really know everything? A look into the prophecies of the Old Testament will give us a clue about God's perfect knowledge. Take a look at just a few of the numerous predictions about the life and death of Jesus Christ made by prophets such as David, Isaiah, Micah, Malachi, Zechariah, and Daniel. If you were to compute the odds of all of those predictions about Jesus coming true, the odds would be more than a billion to one. It would be unrealistic to say that the predictions about Jesus were coincidences; God knew what would take place thousands of years before it happened. This just shows a glimpse of how much God knows.

God knows the complete history of everything from beginning to end because He lives outside the scope of time.

Can God Know All?

Since God is the source of all truth, what does that mean for you? It means that you no longer have to wonder what truth really is; you don't have to figure out where to find truth. You simply need to get in touch with the One who knows the truth. Go back to the conversation Jesus had with Pilate, and you'll find an amazing statement that should give you hope in establishing truth in your life. Jesus told Pilate that He came into the world to bring truth to the world. (See John 18:37.) You don't have to wander in the darkness trying to figure out truth. Jesus came to point you to truth.

So does that mean that Christians know the complete truth? If a Christian turns to God, will that person know everything because he or she knows God? No. Christians are not given a complete picture of reality when they place their faith in Christ. But we are given access to the completeness of truth. Your source of truth is not defined by culture, a bunch of textbooks, your supervisor, your parents, or even yourself. Your source of truth is God. It is like getting a library card. You have access to an abundance of knowledge, but by no means do you possess all of that knowledge. You will find the truth you need to live your life in a relationship with God, the author and possessor of truth.

The dilemma is that although people want to know truth, they do not want to submit to its source—they don't want to live under God's authority.

Truth and Consequences

People falsely believe they can find an alternate source of truth outside of God. They listen to what culture, their friends, the media, or even their own intellects say is truth. Sadly, by taking God out of the equation, we are left with relative truth, which is no truth at all. The fact is that God is the source of truth, whether or not we like it or choose to build our lives on it.

The problem is that humanity has rebelled against God's authority as the author of truth. Why? Because we foolishly think we know more than God. Our attitude is that we know better than God and we can figure out our own way without God. We think we can do just fine in our lives without God's help and without God's control in our lives. It's been that way since

Adam and Eve sinned in the garden of Eden. (Check out Gen. 3.) We want truth but don't want to go to its source to find it. As a result, people read, think, argue, meditate, and deprive themselves to attain truth on their own. But the result will always be the same. Those who search for truth outside of God will always come up short, like drinking dirt when you're thirsty—it only makes things worse.

You are entering a world that is often hostile to the truth as presented in the Bible. People you encounter may try to lure you into a debate about truth because they think that if they can disprove God as the source of truth, they can validate their own faulty understanding of truth. If they can prove that God is not the author of truth, then they can choose to find truth wherever they want, even if it's not really truth at all.

Getting Close to the Truth

If truth can be known and truth is found in God, then how do you know what truths to build your life on? Simple. You get close to the One who holds the truth. By being closer to God, His truths become clearer to us. In the same way, our distance from God leads to doubts about the truth of God.

Think about it this way. Can you remember a time in your relationship with God when you were really close to Him? Maybe it was a summer at camp or on a mission trip. You were more secure in your beliefs and understanding of God and His plan for your life. Now think about a time in your life when you weren't close to God, when you weren't spending time in His Word or with other Christians. You probably questioned God and His plan for you, and your actions showed it. You rebelled against Him. You chose to live apart from the truth of God because you weren't close to Him.

Our distance from God leads to doubts about the truth of God.

What steps can we take to keep in close contact with the source of truth that guides our lives? Communicate with Him regularly. Prayer is such an amazing tool that God gave us; at any time and in any place, we can call on God and know He hears us. Studying the Bible is another step we can take. The Bible should never be treated like a magic answer book, but we can go to it to discover the truths that God has made clear through the letters and narratives of the Bible. Building relationships with other believers is a great way to grow closer to God. We can speak with people who have learned more, grown more mature, and have been grounded in the truths that we have yet to discover.

Satan is subtle. He will tell you that the Bible is outdated, that prayer is a vain exercise, and that religion is merely a crutch for the weak.

The Enemy of Truth

Sounds easy, right? Just stay close to God and you'll know the truth you need to build your life upon. The problem is that we have a powerful enemy whose purpose is to distort, ridicule, and confuse the truths of God. Since the garden of Eden, the devil has been trying to confuse people into thinking that truth is whatever you want it to be, that there are no absolute truths. He turned Eve against God by convincing her that God's truth was not absolute and that it was not for her benefit. (See Gen. 3:1-6.) Look around and you will clearly see hostility toward the truth of God. Think about how people treat God's ideal for sex, families, relationships, and life itself. People are almost defiant in their denial of truth in the face of a God who longs to protect them from themselves.

Satan is subtle. He will tell you that the Bible is outdated, that prayer is a vain exercise, and that religion is merely a crutch for the weak. However, without a standard of truth in your life, everything becomes relative to the individual or the circumstances. You may even be able to see this in your own life. Church may have become boring, your commitment to study God's Word may have diminished, and your stance on "black and white" issues is now looking a lot more gray.

In John 10:10, Jesus described Satan as the "thief" who comes to do three things: steal, kill, and destroy. In fact, 1 Peter 5:8 says that the enemy longs to devour you like a lion devours its prey. You have an enemy who is bent on your total destruction. He wants you to deny God and deny His authority in your life as the basis of truth. To turn against truth found in God is to offer your life as a playground in which Satan destroys your life.

Guided by Truth

Why should you cherish the truth of God? Because a person will act upon the truths he or she believes. For example, a person cheats on a test because on some level, he has disregarded the truth that cheating is wrong. A person may treat others with cruelty because she has created a truth for herself that the harmed person does not deserve justice. Whether we understand it or not, the truths you build your life on will determine your ethics and your actions.

The person who is resistant to the truth of God or ignores that truth will live a life with ever-changing rules of right and wrong. He will follow his desires and will justify anything that furthers his efforts or his version of truth. On the other hand, the one who agrees with God about truth accepts the unchanging standards of truth gained by a relationship with God. And that life is more amazing than you and I could ever imagine.

Truth demands that we abandon our own plan for our lives and live according to God's good plan for us. It demands that we give God control of our lives, and most of us don't want to do that.

Truth 101

Now that we know that God is the source of truth and He wants us to live in truth, what are some truths of God that we can live by? First, we need to understand that God is an eternal, omniscient (all-knowing), and loving God. He knows everything, but we won't know everything. At times, God will call us to trust Him in an area even when we don't know all the answers. We may not know what God is up to. We may not see how He is working things out, but we know enough about God to know that we can trust Him even when we don't know all the answers.

Second, we need to understand that we can trust the Bible to provide the basis for truth. Relying on God's knowledge and using the Bible as our guide, we can base our lives on a few important truths:

1. *God is the Creator and Sustainer of all.* He has created humanity to live in relationship with Him.
2. *God has set forth a standard for living, a standard for right and wrong.*

Violating that standard (which is called sinning) creates consequences—
separation from God. Sin causes a rift in the relationship with God.

3. *God could not bear to leave humanity in a state of separation from Himself.*
   That's why He came to earth in spite of our rebellion.
4. *The sacrifice of Jesus has opened the door for humanity to be reconciled
   to God.* Because of Jesus, we can enjoy a restored relationship with God
   and an eternity with Him in heaven.

Why Fear Truth?

What is so scary about these truths? Truth demands that we abandon
our own plan for our lives and live according to God's good plan for us. It
demands that we give God control of our lives, and most of us don't want
to do that. We want life on our terms, not His terms, even though His way
is better. Many people would rather struggle through life without God's
peace, purpose, and leadership than to choose to follow Him.

Walk Away or Run To?

Pilate walked away after asking Jesus "What is truth?" And he walked out
on Jesus before finding out the answer. Something tells me that Jesus would
not have hesitated to share with Pilate the truth he so deeply desired if
Pilate had been willing to listen. You have the same choice as Pilate. You
can choose to listen to God's truth, or you can walk away.

Extra Credit

- Find the "Comparative Religions Chart" on the CD-ROM under the section
  "Defending Your Faith." Spend some time discovering the beliefs of the
  major religions in our world. Compare those beliefs to the truths found
  in God's Word.
- Check out the Web links and articles on the CD-ROM. They can provide
  you with some great information about other religions and defending your
  faith. These will be valuable resources as you encounter others who do
  not share your same beliefs.

The distinction between Christianity and all other systems of religion consists largely in this: that in these other, men are found seeking after God, while Christianity is God seeking after men. —Thomas Arnold

Chapter 3

THE GROUND BENEATH THE WALK

On Saturday morning, April 26, 2003, Aron Ralston left his truck at the trail head of Horseshoe Canyon. He was looking forward to a day of hiking and canyoneering around the Blue John Canyon in Utah. An experienced mountaineer, Aron had made last-minute plans for his five-day vacation. In his hurry to get out of town and having not made specific plans of his whereabouts, Aron did not tell his family or friends where he was going. Only hours after scaling rocks and canyons, the ground beneath his walk shifted. More specifically, a half-ton boulder that had been lodged for years gave way and trapped his arm. In Ralston's own words: "I feel the stone respond to my adjusting grip with a quake. Instantly, I know this is trouble, and instinctively I let go of the rotating boulder to land on the round rocks on the canyon floor. I look up, and the backlit chockstone consumes the sky. Fear shoots my hands over my head. I can't move backwards or I'll fall over a small ledge.

"The next three seconds play out in slow motion. The falling rock smashes my left hand against the south wall; I yank my left arm back as the rock ricochets in the confined space; the boulder then crushes my right hand, thumb up, fingers extended; the rock slides another foot down the wall with my arm in tow, tearing the skin off the lateral side of my forearm. Then, silence."[1]

Remarkably, Ralston survived his six-day ordeal of being trapped. But it did not end without serious consequences. After days of dehydration and calculating his options, Ralston did the unthinkable—he amputated his own arm with a crude pocket knife and walked several miles out of the canyon until rescuers found him. His stamina, knowledge, and experience had given him a foundation to survive an unthinkable trauma.

Like Ralston, before you leave on the adventure after high school called "life," you must have a strong foundation of spiritual disciplines to guide you through unchartered territory. You will face boulders and shifting circumstances, but you can weather the future if you start with the right foundation. Jesus said, "Therefore, everyone who hears these words of Mine and acts on them will be like a sensible man who built his house on the rock. The rain fell, the rivers rose, and the winds blew and pounded that house. Yet it didn't collapse, because its foundation was on the rock" (Matt. 7:24-25). Jesus said there were two different ways to build—the right way which is on a solid rock or the wrong way which is on a shifting foundation of sand. Which will you choose?

Without first having a personal relationship with Christ, any attempt to build a strong foundation for your life is futile.

Fixed to the Rock

A good builder begins construction on a house by first laying a cornerstone. A *cornerstone* is a stone in the foundation that forms a part of a corner or angle in a wall. Ancient builders used a cornerstone as the starting point and would level or square the rest of a building by this one stone. This foundation is crucial. It is the key to successful building. If you don't have a good foundation, you're in trouble (just ask folks in California who built their houses along fault lines). In your spiritual life, you must have a solid and secure foundation—a relationship to Christ, who is the cornerstone of faith.

The Apostle Peter wrote: "Look! I lay a stone in Zion, a chosen and valuable cornerstone, and the one who believes in Him will never be put to shame!" (1 Pet. 2:6). Without first having a personal relationship with Christ, any attempt to build a strong foundation for your life is futile.

Train Yourself in Godliness

If you've ever participated in athletics, you understand the importance of physical training. When a game is close and the competition is tough, usually the team in the best physical shape can outlast the team that did not make training a priority. Any coach will tell you that long-lasting physical stamina is not obtained overnight, but over a long period of time. The same applies to spiritual strength as well. In fact, it's not a coincidence that the words *disciple* and *discipline* are so similar. Being a disciple of Christ takes great discipline and time. In 1 Timothy 4:7, Paul wrote, "train yourself in godliness." The Greek word translated "train" is *gumnazo*. The words *gymnasium* and *gymnastics* come from this word. Paul was instructing young Timothy to "work out" his spiritual training until he reached the goal. The goal of physical training is good for the body, but the value of godliness is greater. Following Jesus is a day-by-day, even moment-by-moment process of dedication to spiritual growth. Growth does not happen by itself.

Abiding in Christ

Think about the following statement: You become like the people you have chosen to follow. Dallas Willard wrote, "One thing is for sure. You are somebody's disciple. You learned how to live from somebody else. There are no exceptions to this rule, for human beings are just the kind of creatures that have to learn and keep learning from others how to live."[2] Even if you think you are your "own person," your beliefs and values are developed in part from people you have chosen to follow. Think about it for a moment. Who are some people you have followed in the past or follow today? What were they like? The way you think, act, and feel has been shaped by those people. It may have been your parents, a friend who led you astray, or even a youth worker. But make no mistake—you become like the person you choose to follow.

If you are shaped by those you follow, how do you become a fully devoted follower of Christ? First, it takes commitment on your part. Do you really want to "grow up" spiritually? Many Christians are still spiritual babies no matter their physical age. You may have been a Christian for 10 years but you act like a spiritual baby. Hebrews 5:14 encourages spiritual maturity, "But solid food is for the mature—for those whose senses have been trained to distinguish between good and evil."

So what are the steps in growing up in your faith, becoming more like your Lord? The key is abiding in Christ. So what does that mean? To abide means to remain stable or fixed in something. It means to stick with it, to continue in it over a long time. You remain in God by sticking to reading your Bible and sticking to prayer.

Abiding in His Word

In today's world, God's Word is more available than ever before, but most people are clueless about what the Bible has to say. Even many Christians choose not to spend time in God's Word, which nourishes your soul and strengthens your relationship with God. Just as an anorexic person refuses nourishment from food, many Christians refuse the daily nourishment from God's Word. And as a result, they are spiritually anorexic.

So how do you feed on God's Word? Look at an acrostic for the word *heart* for some tips.

H—HEARING God's Word

To learn and abide in God's Word you need to hear it. You hear it when you attend church and listen to someone preach from the Bible. That's one of the reasons it will be vitally important for you to be involved in a local church after you complete high school. Not only do you need the fellowship and accountability of other Christians, but you also need to hear God's Word on a consistent basis. It also will be important for you to choose where you hear God's Word—make sure what is being preached and taught is the complete, trustworthy Word of God.

"I think having a quiet time was the most important spiritual foundation I learned while I was in student ministry." — Claire, age 19

E—EXAMINING God's Word

Hearing God's Word at church is not enough. That's like eating a meal only once a week. You also need to spend time examining God's Word through personal quiet times and study opportunities. Why? Because God uses His Word to communicate directly to you! In fact, the Bible is not just a book of stories and guidelines for living. Hebrews 4:12 says, "The word of God is living and effective and sharper than any two-edged sword, penetrating as far as to divide soul, spirit, joints, and marrow; it is a judge of the ideas and thoughts of the heart." God's Word works deep in your heart, penetrating and changing you from the inside out!

After high school, one of the tests you will face is choosing when and where you spend time alone with God. If you go to college, you will probably face the temptation of sleeping in until the last minute when you race off to class. Even if you don't go to college, you will face the temptation of staying up late and hanging out with friends or goofing off instead of hanging out with God. The only way to keep grounded in God's Word and have a quiet time is to make it part of your daily routine—the same place, the same time, the same goal of being with God.

Another way you spend time examining God's Word is through Bible studies with other Christians. They will hold you accountable and challenge you to explore the Bible in deeper ways than you could on your own. Find a Bible study on campus or in your church. If you can't find a group to join at the moment, look for Bible studies that you can work through on your own. Just don't neglect your spiritual diet.

A—APPLYING God's Word

Pretend for a minute that you took an auto repair class in high school. You learned the parts of a car and the tools needed for repair and maintenance. But you didn't really learn anything until you actually got your hands greasy and applied all that knowledge to fix an actual car.

Applying God's Word is a lot like that. In James 1:22, Christians are encouraged to "be doers of the word and not hearers only." In other words, don't just tell me what you know; show me by your actions. John 15:8 describes spiritual growth as producing fruit. You can hear Scripture and even study it, but until it results in changes your life, you are not really moving forward in your spiritual growth.

R—REMEMBERING God's Word

As a child, you may have learned verses in Sunday School or Vacation Bible School. Part of abiding in God's Word is having God's Word abide in you. But have you continued the practice of Scripture memory? How will you continue once you leave high school? Hiding God's Word in your heart (see Ps. 119:11) will help you resist temptation, give you boldness in sharing your witness for Christ, and give you comfort during trials and temptations. For help in this area, check out the "Scripture Memory Cards" and "Scripture Memory 101" on your CD-ROM.

T—THINKING on God's Word

Thinking on God's Word, or meditating on it, is the final part of learning how to abide in Scripture. Philippians 4:8 sums this up, "Finally brothers, whatever is true, whatever is honorable, whatever is just, whatever is pure, whatever is lovely, whatever is commendable—if there is any moral excellence and if there is any praise—dwell on these things." If you want God's Word to transform your life, make it a habit to daily reflect on Scripture. Repeat verses as you memorize them, asking God to reveal new things that will draw you closer to Him.

Personal Testimony

During my freshman year of college, I had the opportunity to take a month-long class that emphasized Scripture memory. Our professor announced the stipulation for passing the class—memorize 180 verses in three weeks! Dr. Bettis gave us specific instructions on how to prepare our verses on note cards, listing both the verse and the reference.

At the end of three weeks I entered a classroom with many other students who accepted the challenge. With an empty blue book and several pencils in my hand, I started writing God's Word. Verse after verse came—one right after another. For almost three hours I sat at the desk and continued to write as God brought Scripture to my mind. The result? I wrote 220 verses of Scripture in my own handwriting. It was one of the most incredible spiritual experiences of my life. That three-week course was a spiritual marker for me and helped give me a solid foundation of the spiritual discipline of memorizing Scripture.

Abiding in Prayer

Now that you know how to abide in God's Word using the simple acrostic for *heart*, let's explore a way you can talk to Him. Simply put, prayer is talking to God. With whom do you share your deepest thoughts? Is there someone you long to talk to every day? Praying to God is a lot like that. It is your conversation time with Him. He's someone with whom you can share your deepest desires, confess your deepest secrets, and express your frustrations and hurts. Abiding in Christ through prayer is experiencing His presence during your entire day. The Apostle Paul even encouraged believers to "pray constantly" (1 Thess. 5:17). Paul was not saying you must drop everything in your life and pray; he was encouraging believers to remain in an attitude of knowing Christ is with you at any hour of the day and He is available to hear your prayers. So how do you develop the spiritual foundation of prayer? Use this simple outline:

1. Praise God for who He is. Repeat Scripture back to Him. Acknowledge God's presence in your life.
2. Go to God with sin, confess it specifically, and then repent. To repent means to turn the other direction and not turn back.
3. Tell God about the important things you're facing right now— whether you need help in a job interview, guidance in a relationship, or the discipline to study for an upcoming test. He is concerned about every detail of your life. Also spend time talking about other people—people who need His help, who are hurting, or who need to know Him.
4. Submit to God's authority in your life. He may speak to your heart, telling you about something you may need to do as a result of spending time with Him. Just as you slow down on the road when you see a yield sign, look for ways God wants you to yield to Him.

Extra Credit

• Begin a prayer journal. Record the day you make your request and the day it is answered. Out to the side of the request, write down how God answered. Keep track of your prayer journal for six weeks and look back at how God has revealed Himself to you. Spend one day thanking God for answering all your requests and pray in confidence for the ones He hasn't yet answered.

• Find an accountability partner who will challenge you to memorize at least one verse of Scripture each week for the next two months. If you need help determining which Scriptures to memorize, print the "Scripture Memory Cards" from your CD-ROM. They can be found in the section "The Christian Walk."

1. Aron Ralston, *Between a Rock and a Hard Place* (New York: Atria Books, 2004), 23.
2. Dallas Willard, *The Divine Conspiracy* (San Francisco: HarperSanFrancisco, 1997), 272.

Home is a mighty test of character.
What you are at home you are everywhere,
whether you demonstrate it or not.
—Thomas DeWitt Talmadge

Chapter 4

THE TIDES OF CHANGE

As a child, did you ever go to the beach? Did you chase the tide as it rolled in and out across the sand? Did you build a sand castle? Did you go back the next morning to find that it had washed away in the night tide? Change can seem a lot like the tides. Sometimes change comes in like the neap tide—slow, gradual, and expected. Other times change comes in like an unexpected tidal wave. Either way, change happens. It is a natural part of the rhythm of life. But you can deal with change a little easier if you prepare for it.

Neap tide—a tide, occurring twice a month, when high tide is at its lowest level.

The Neap Tide

Ella grew up in a town with a great junior college. She decided to spend the first two years there so she could be close to home and save some money. Then she would transfer to a four-year college and finish her degree. After making preparations to move into the dorm, she left home and had a pretty easy transition into college life. Her family was 45 minutes up the road, and all of her close friends were at school with her. A neap tide—a slow, gradual transition.

The Tidal Wave

Antonio had done well in high school and thought he'd get financial help to go away to college. But that didn't happen. So he agreed to live at home and attend the college in town to help save money. As high school graduation approached, all seemed well. He was accepted into the local college and had a job he could keep during school. His parents were excited about him staying at home; they liked having him around. But less than a month after graduation, his parents moved 10 hours away. Huge change—like a tidal wave.

Tidal wave—a very large, damaging wave, caused by an earthquake or very strong wind.

How can you deal with the tides of change after graduation? A lot of things will change in your life when you get that magic piece of paper called a diploma. One major area of change will be in your family. You'll learn how to relate to each other in different ways as you become more mature, and as your family learns to see you as an adult. Be patient, though. It will take all of your family working together to avoid the undertow of the tides.

Undertow—a strong current beneath the surface of water and in a different direction.

What Is Going On?

You are a senior, probably 18 and "legal," and your parents still want input in your decisions and life. Is that fair? How much parental involvement do you still need or want? How can you reach an agreement on the issues that you see differently? Should they let you make your own decisions and live with the consequences? Do you argue with them, ignore their advice and instructions, and do whatever it takes to be away from the house? Desiring independence is normal, but it is not an excuse for poor behavior on your part. Your family is making major adjustments, so it is no wonder that the tides are rolling in and out at home. What is going on?

Tide 1—Choices and Decisions. You're trying to make decisions on your own. For some decisions, you need your parents' help and input, but others you need to make on your own. This can be frustrating on both sides because you and your parents will have different opinions on when you need advice and how much. It's a learning process that unfortunately causes much tension.

Tide 2—Separation Anxiety. You may be preparing to leave home, and you and your parents are beginning to make that adjustment emotionally. As a senior, it's OK for you to be a little sad about moving away from home. (It's also OK to be excited, too, even in the midst of the sadness.)

Tide 3—Choosing to Stay at Home. If you choose to stay at home after graduation (whether you're working or going to college), you will still face adjustments. Life as an adult is different from going to high school, and you may face some conflicts as a result. Keep in mind, though, that if you choose to stay at home, you should still be taking on financial responsibilities as well as helping around the house. Discuss the specifics and come to an agreement.

If you choose to stay at home, you should still be taking on financial responsibilities.

Tide 4—Social Life. Close friends may be going to different schools or choosing paths that will take them away. Enjoy your time with your friends before graduation. However, overloading on social activity during your senior year can add more stress.

Tide 5—Academic Expectations. As scholarship and graduation deadlines approach, the anxiety often increases. Rejection can often lead to past regrets and increased tension. And this will often lead to stress and anxiety at home as you and your parents worry about the future.

Tide 6—Financial Obligations. Paying for college or preparing to live on your own can be quite expensive. You need to be working toward financial independence, but you may still need some help from your parents, especially if you are in school full-time.

With all these dynamics influencing your family, it's no wonder that your family is changing. Navigating all the tides of change can be frustrating and scary. The good news is that God provides some principles that will help you navigate through these changes.

Avoid the Tidal Wave: What Does God Say?

The Bible states it bluntly in Exodus 20:12. God gave His people principles to live by, and one of those simply states: Honor your father and your mother.

"Honor your father and your mother so that you may have a long life in the land that the Lord your God is giving you" (Ex. 20:12).

3 4

Teens offer a lot of excuses for not honoring their parents. Have you ever heard these comments (or said them yourself)? "They don't understand me." "They're old and don't remember what it was like to be 18." "I'm an adult now. I don't have to obey." "They aren't Christians." "They're just being overprotective. I know what I'm doing."

Sorry to burst your bubble, but there are no conditions attached to honoring and obeying your parents. (The only exception is if they ask you to do something sinful.) However, God does promise that if you obey Him (and your parents), He will bless you.

Be More Specific, Please

What does it mean to honor your father and mother? It means developing an inward respect for your parents. You won't agree with every decision they make or try to get you to make, but you can respect their opinions and appreciate their good intentions. Parents usually want only what is best for their teenager. Listen to what your parents are really saying, not what you think they are saying.

Honoring your parents means showing respect in your actions. This applies to eye rolling, foot tapping, snide remarks under your breath, hair flipping, and walking away. Look at your parents while they are talking and respond occasionally to let them know you are still with them. This can be almost impossible to do when you are disagreeing with them, but give it your best effort. Interrupting them will not make your case any better, so wait until they are finished and then calmly say what you have on your mind.

Does honoring and obeying your parents mean you can't disagree or discuss the issue with them? Absolutely not. It shows maturity on your part to initiate a conversation about issues with which you don't agree or understand. Most arguments come from miscommunication of ideas, feelings, or expectations. A calm, intelligent discussion can often clear up misconceptions, and you and your parents can reach a mutual agreement. Fair warning: this doesn't mean that they will always change their minds.

Most arguments come from miscommunication of ideas, feelings, or expectations.

God granted Solomon (the writer of many of the Proverbs) extraordinary wisdom. He was quite clear about the importance of listening to your parents. Read some things this wise man said:

Listen, my son, to your father's instruction, and don't reject your mother's teaching. —Proverbs 1:8

A fool despises his father's instruction, but a person who heeds correction is sensible. —Proverbs 15:5

Listen to your father who gave you life, and don't despise your mother when she is old. —Proverbs 23:22

As a senior, you are in transition. In some ways you are like the tides, somewhat predictable and usually easy to deal with. But admit it—sometimes you can pull a tidal wave on your parents. You aren't a child anymore, but you aren't an adult either. You have more responsibilities and influences in your life than ever before, but you still need support from your parents—spiritually, financially, and emotionally—whether you want to admit it or not!

How Long?

You've been waiting all your life to be on your own and to make your own decisions. It may come as a surprise to you, but your parents have been waiting for the same thing. One of their goals is to see you become a responsible, decision-making adult who can live independently. One of the greatest ways for you to honor your parents is by being capable of making decisions that reflect the biblical values you've been taught.

For the rest of your life, you are to honor your parents. Your relationship with your parents will continue to change. What makes this phase so uncomfortable and sometimes downright miserable is that it is a new situation that neither you nor your parents have experienced before. You want freedom; they still want control. They want to give you responsibility; you don't always want it. You want to be treated as an adult; they still see you as their "child." But no matter what your age, God still wants you to honor your parents.

What makes this phase so uncomfortable and sometimes downright miserable is that it is a new situation that neither you nor your parents have experienced before.

Parents 101

Whether you have the greatest relationship or a roller-coaster relationship with your parents, you can all do some practical things during the senior year and after graduation to encourage a stronger, healthier relationship. You may be considering college, a career, military service, or marriage. Whatever you choose, your relationship with your parents is going to change over the next year or two. Gear up and get ready!

1. *Mend relationships before you leave home.* You may need to take the initiative, but it will be worth it. Leaving home is tough anyway, and a rocky relationship will only make it more difficult. Don't count on the problem going away once you leave; it seldom does.

2. *Spend time with your immediate and extended family.* Attend the family reunion you've managed to avoid for the last few years. Plan outings for you and your siblings. Do something special with each parent or guardian. Stay home occasionally on a weekend and just hang out. Attend church regularly with your family.

3. *Stay in touch after you leave.* E-mail or actually mail a note or picture home. Call parents, siblings, and grandparents regularly. They know you are busy and don't have time for long, detailed conversations; they just want to know you are OK. Reassure them. Hint: It's a lot easier to ask for a favor if you've stayed in touch.

4. *Prepare for the transition together.* Discuss the arrangements for moving out. Listen to your parents' advice and suggestions. They may allow you to make the choices, but they may also have some wise suggestions that

will save you grief later on. Shop for furniture and supplies together. This is one of the last big things they will do with you and for you. Let them enjoy giving this to you.

They may allow you to make the choices, but they may also have some wise suggestions that will save you grief later on.

Think back to the tides at the beach. Although you may have been caught off balance as the sands sifted under your feet, you learned to adjust and enjoy the experience. God has provided you with family to help you when you lose your footing or fall. Continue to honor and respect your family and find joy in this experience as well.

Extra Credit

• Make a card for your parents to give as a surprise to them. Suggested topics include voicing appreciation, offering an apology, suggesting doing something together, or giving them a gift certificate for doing a non-required chore.

My church calls me to her heart. She asks my service and my loyalty. She has a right to ask it! I will help her do for others what she has done for me. In this place in which I live, I will help her keep aflame and aloft the torch of a living faith. —Anonymous

Chapter 5

KEEPING THE CONNECTION

3 9

Have you ever broken a bone before? One winter while playing basketball with a group of teenagers, I was reaching for a loose ball under the basket. Stretching out to get the ball, my hand hit the hardwood floor—hard. I continued to play the game thinking that I had only sprained my hand. The next morning I woke up and my hand was as big as a balloon. I knew at that time something was definitely wrong. I had broken a bone in my hand that required surgery. For several weeks I had to adjust the way I did things. I had to shower and dress differently. I had to eat differently. Even driving was a bit crazy for a while. I learned through my weeks of recovery that I took the use of my right hand for granted. I just wasn't able to do things like I could with the use of both hands.

It is important that you stay connected to your church family whether you are going to college, going into the workforce, or joining the military.

Just as the hands are important to the physical body, so are the legs, feet, eyes, ears, and nose. They all work in coordination with one another. Each body part has a purpose, a function, but all are dependent on one another.

Just as my hand has an important function in my life, you have a significant role in your local church. It is important that you stay connected to your church family whether you are going to college, going into the workforce, or joining the military. You will need continual encouragement and accountability from a church family in the coming years, and a church family will need you and your gifts. Without you, the church won't function as it's designed.

New Freedoms Ahead

It has been said that the college years are a lot like the "twilight zone." You have not experienced anything like it up to this point, and you will not experience anything like it after you graduate from college. Even if you're not going to college, these years are nothing like you've ever known. You will experience a lot of freedoms you did not have in high school. The attendance office won't call your parents if you skip classes or ditch work. You won't be held to a school dress code to make sure you are wearing appropriate clothing. There won't always be someone to help you keep a balanced schedule of mental, physical, and spiritual health.

Make no mistake. Your involvement in God's family matters. Your life counts. God wants to use you in significant ways as a young adult.

You have waited most of your life to experience some of these things. However, your spiritual walk may suffer if these new freedoms lead you to neglect your relationship with Jesus and the local church. You may even be tempted to offer excuses for neglecting your role in a local body of believers, the church. You might hear your friends say something like, "The only time I get to sleep in is on Sunday morning." Others might say, "I've had to go to church all my life. Now it's my turn to do what I want to do without my parents being in my face." Or you may think, *The church doesn't really need me. I don't really count.* But make no mistake. Your involvement in God's family matters. Your life counts.

Unity Brings Encouragement

As you make the transition from the youth group into adulthood, you will need encouragement to continue growing spiritually. You may be moving away and need to establish new friendships and a new church family. You may be staying in your hometown and home church because of a job opportunity. Whatever the case, you need the encouragement of your church family as much as your church family needs you.

The writer of Hebrews provides some insight into the need for staying connected to other Christians in the church. "Let us hold on to the confession of our hope without wavering, for He who promised is faithful. And let us be concerned about one another in order to promote love and good works, not staying away from our meetings, as some habitually do, but encouraging each other, and all the more as you see the day drawing near" (Heb. 10:23-25).

Whether you go away or stay home to attend college, begin a full-time job, or enter into the military service from high school, the church is your lifeline for spiritual growth. You will need the church and it will need you.

41

"Making a commitment to be involved and serving is the best way I have found to stay connected to the church." —Codi, 22

Your Foot Isn't a Hand

In 1 Corinthians 12:12-31, the Apostle Paul wrote about the importance of the body of Christ. The physical body functions with many different members and organs, yet those parts form one body. Christians make up the body of Christ, the church. From the newest believer to the Christian who has been in the church family for years, all are equal and all are important to the work of the church. You are important to God in His church and are needed in the life and work of the church.

Did you know that your ability to keep your balance, walk a straight line, and weave in and out of a crowd is very dependent on your big toe? But if you don't have a foot to put the big toe on, what good is it? What if you didn't have the leg to attach the foot to? Get the picture? God created our physical bodies interdependent on the individual parts.

How ridiculous would it be if your foot decided to take a permanent vacation because it wasn't as visible as a hand? What if your ear decided to stop working because it didn't feel important, like the heart or an eye? This mentality marks many Christians. Because they are not the pastor, youth minister, or a deacon, they don't think they matter. They don't think God can use their skills and gifts. But this passage in 1 Corinthians 12 makes it clear that all members of the body of Christ (the church) need one another—high school graduates included.

4 2

How ridiculous would it be if your foot decided to take a permanent vacation because it wasn't as visible as a hand?

Gifts from the Spirit

So how do you know you're gifted to be used by God? Simple. Scripture tells us. Every person who has placed his or her trust in Christ has been given a spiritual gift (which is different from a talent) that God can use to build up the church and draw people to a relationship with Christ. So what are some spiritual gifts? Glad you asked. Romans 12:6-8, Ephesians 4:11, 1 Corinthians 12:8-10,28-30 , and 1 Peter 4:9-11 list the following gifts:

- Prophecy
- Faith
- Service/helps
- Healing
- Teaching
- Apostleship

- Giving
- Discernment
- Leadership
- Hospitality
- Mercy
- Wisdom

- Shepherding
- Knowledge
- Administration
- Exhortation (Encouragement)
- Evangelism

For more information about these spiritual gifts, check out the information on your CD-ROM. It contains a spiritual gift test to help you determine your gifts, along with an explanation of how each of these gifts is used in the church.

Every person who has placed his or her trust in Christ has been given a spiritual gift (which is different from a talent) that God can use to build up the church and draw people to a relationship with Christ.

What spiritual gift(s) do you have? How can you serve effectively in the body of Christ? Remember that the purpose of these gifts is to lift up Christ and to build up His body, the church. Even though there are different spiritual gifts, there is only one Spirit of God at work through those gifts. The gifts may have different results, but they have one common purpose—to lift up Christ and build up the church.

Keep in mind that we do not choose which spiritual gifts God gives us. The Holy Spirit is the source of all spiritual gifts. God chooses how He will gift you. There is no room in the body of Christ for envy, division, or pride when it comes to spiritual gifts.

There is no room in the body of Christ for envy, division, or pride when it comes to spiritual gifts.

You may not recognize you have gifts. Sometimes gifts get buried because of a cold or distant personal relationship with God. Gifts are misunderstood, distorted, misused, and even ignored. To use your gifts in service for God, you must recognize them, understand them, develop them, and find appropriate ways to use them in ministry. First Peter 4:10 reminds us, "Based on the gift they have received, everyone should use it to serve others, as good managers of the varied grace of God."

Someone's Watching You

OK, so you know God has gifted you. The body of Christ needs your service. So is that the only reason you should be involved in the church beyond high school? Nope. There's another reason—your influence on the people around you. You may not realize it, but people young and old are watching you. Adults who are watching you might be thinking, *Is that student going to be successful in whatever she attempts beyond high school?* Children are wondering, *Is he still going to come to church now that he isn't living* at home and his parents aren't there to make him or remind him to come? First Timothy 4:12 is a good challenge for you. It says that, "No one should despise your youth; instead, you should be an example to the believers in speech, in conduct, in love, in faith, in purity." In other words, your life should be a living example to those around you.

I always looked up to the older youth in my church. They seemed to always be doing something for Jesus. When I entered the youth group, I was disappointed when students gained their independence and dropped their commitment to church. My goal as a high school sophomore is to be one who stays the course and continues to be used by God in my junior, senior, and college years. —Angela, 16

Consider those who look up to you as a role model and those who have encouraged you during your high school years. Could this be a time in your life when you could give back to your church? Make that commitment to stay connected to a church no matter if you are away at college, home for college, entering the workforce, or in the military. Unfortunately only a small percentage of high school seniors stay connected to church after graduation. Your commitment to Christ and the ministries of the church will determine whether you will stay connected.

If you are headed for military service, you may want to seek an active, mature Christian in your home church to be an accountability partner with you while serving away from home. You could keep in contact with each other by e-mail and/or regular mail. That mentor can be praying specifically for you and asking you the tough questions about your walk with Christ.

Unfortunately only a small percentage of high school seniors stay connected to church after graduation. Your commitment to Christ and the ministries of the church will determine whether you will stay connected.

If you are going into the workforce directly from high school, you may have opportunity to be more involved in your church than you were in the past. While in high school, you spent a lot of time and effort in your studies or extracurricular activities. Now you can invest this time in your church. You can work with preschoolers or children. Do yard work. Sing. Paint. Fold bulletins. The opportunities are endless. Just remember: your life matters. Don't waste it!

Extra Credit

- Talk with your pastor, student minister, or Baptist Campus minister. Ask about his calling into ministry and what spiritual gifts he has that are beneficial to him in ministry.
- Visit a Baptist Campus Ministry. Discover ways you can be involved in ministry beyond high school.
- Find at least one younger youth that you can mentor through his or her high school years.
- If you will live away from your current church after high school, access the Church Search Web site (listed on the CD-ROM) to locate Southern Baptist churches near where you will be living. And get involved!

We have to live but one day
at a time, but we are living
for eternity in that one day.
—Anonymous

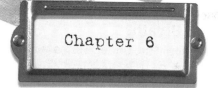

Chapter 6

TIME CRUNCH

T ommy died. It happened more than 15 years ago, but I remember it like it happened just a few minutes ago. The phone rang. I answered it, and our neighbor on the other end of the line asked if Tommy's car was parked in his driveway across the street from us. I looked out the window and told her it was not there. She said she heard that something bad had happened to Tommy. It turns out she was right. Tommy had been killed less than an hour earlier.

We had been friends for more than 10 years. Tommy was a few years older than I, but we lived across the street from each other, so we became friends. When we were both in high school we weren't as close as we had been, but we had made some great memories over the years. Now he was dead. It was just a week or so before prom. He was on the way to pick up his prom date to take her to get her dress when he took a curve too fast and lost control.

You probably have known someone close to your age who has died (or at least heard about it). It happens every week—so often we've become numb to it. It may affect us for a while, but life goes on.

Wouldn't it be great if you could know when your time on earth would end? Or would it be great? Would you live differently? Whether you live to be 18 or 80, your time is short. You don't know how long your time will be. Make the most of every hour you live!

Do You Have Good Breath?

A person's life expectancy in the United States is 77.4 years. That translates to 678,024 hours of life. Of that time, you can expect to spend 197,215 hours sleeping; 56,347 hours eating; and 28,173 hours involved in personal hygiene in your lifetime. If you add up those numbers, you'll see that close to half of your life (42 percent to be exact) is spent sleeping, eating, and practicing hygiene. If you want your life to matter, you'd better consider carefully what you do with the other 58 percent of your time.

When you reach the age of 18, you will have lived approximately 23 percent of your life.

The psalmist understood the importance of making the most of time. He wrote, "Show me, O Lord, my life's end and the number of my days; let me know how fleeting is my life. You have made my days a mere hand-breadth; the span of my years is as nothing before you. Each man's life is but a breath" (Ps. 39:4-5, NIV).

The Bible says the length of your life is like a breath. In the time it takes you to read this sentence, you will have taken more than one breath. That is short. What are you doing to make the most out of your life?

How Are You Walking?

Enough percentages and numbers. This is not math class. This is life! And you want to live the fullest life possible and get the most out of life. Right? God wants the same for you! He said in Ephesians 5:15-17, "Pay careful attention, then, to how you walk—not as unwise people but as wise—*making the most of the time*, because the days are evil. So don't be foolish, but understand what the Lord's will is." (emphasis added)

So how are you walking? Writing to the church at Ephesus, Paul challenged the people to pay attention to the way they walked. Of course, he didn't care about physical walking—whether you wear sneakers or sandals. He was concerned with being wise, making the most of every opportunity in life.

Make the Most of Every Hour

1. *Live your life knowing you can't recycle time.* Each second that passes is time spent; you cannot get it back. Time machines work only in the fictional world. As you gain more independence and can determine how you invest your time, live with the reality that time cannot be recycled, turned back, or changed.

   It's like toothpaste. Think about what would happen if you bought a new tube of toothpaste, squeezed all of it out into your sink, and then tried to put every bit of it back into the tube. It would practically be impossible to do. You cannot undo what you have done. The same is true of how you spend your time.

   As you live, every moment of your time will either be a waste, a regret, or time well-spent. The time well-spent does not mean that your life will always be an adventure (studying for a chemistry final or showing up to work each day rarely is), but investing your time in things that really matter leaves you with few regrets.

Overcommitment will weaken you. Say no to the good things and say yes to the best things.

2. *Practice saying no.* Life after high school will present you with more opportunities than ever before. You'll have the chance to do many different things, from jobs to classes to hobbies to joining a fraternity or sorority. You'll be bombarded with opportunities. A word of caution: do not do everything that comes your way. Do not take advantage of every opportunity. There is a pressure in our culture to be involved in and good at everything. Overcommitment will weaken you. Say no to the good things and say yes to the best things.

   Cindi Ferrini leads a company called Creative Management Fundamentals. She challenges people to ask themselves the following question when they are faced with an opportunity to do something: "What is my motivation in saying yes?"[1] By evaluating your motivation, you can determine whether or not you're doing something for the wrong reasons. So what are some of these wrong reasons?

   One reason you might agree to a commitment is to try to elevate yourself. Some people agree to do something only to make themselves look good. Life is about God and putting the attention on Him. It's not about you—it's about Him.

A second reason you might say yes to an activity is because other people are doing it. You might want to work in the homeless shelter because volunteering is in and looks good on a job application. Or you might join that fraternity because your roommate is a member. You're an individual person with unique characteristics. Don't let the actions of others dictate yours.

Third, you might want to say yes to an activity in order to impress God. Hosea 6:6 says, "For I desire loyalty and not sacrifice, the knowledge of God rather than burnt offerings." God does not want your sacrifices. He wants your life. He wants you to know Him and have a relationship with Him. Sacrifice will result from your relationship with Him, but God does not want you to do something to earn extra credit or love from Him. It does not work that way.

Life is about God and putting the attention on Him. It's not about you—it's about Him.

3. *Watch for signs of burnout and extreme stress.* When you say yes to too many things, you get stressed out. Long periods of stress turn into burnout. Some signs of stress and burnout include:

Physical	Emotional	Mental
• headaches	• insomnia	• forgetfulness
• indigestion	• moodiness	• loss of concentration
• pimples	• irritability	• disorganization
• tense muscles	• anger	• negative self-talk
• sweaty palms	• lack of humor	• poor judgment

What should you do when you find that you're totally stressed out? First, evaluate your decisions. What can you eliminate from your schedule? Maybe you need to drop a class if you're taking too many hours. Or maybe you don't need to work as many hours. Perhaps you can say no the next time someone needs you to fix a car, baby-sit a child, or mow a lawn. It's OK to say no sometimes. Hopefully this does not come as a shock or insult, but someone else can do what you're doing. Who knows, God may be wanting someone else to do it. By letting go of that responsibility, you are allowing someone else to be used by God.

Second, talk to God. He cares for you. Tell Him that you are giving Him your stresses. You may need to do this every day or several times a day—anytime you feel yourself putting the stress back on yourself.

Third, take action to relieve your stress. The more you internalize stress, the more it will eat away at you. Talk to a friend, take steps to eat healthier, take a walk, or do something fun.

As you get older, more people will rely on you and expect specific things from you. Procrastination makes you appear lazy and unfocused.

4. *Don't procrastinate.* Don't put off your responsibilities until the last minute. Procrastination is harmful in two ways. First, it sabotages you. It teaches you to be lazy and unfocused. Most people will do anything to make their lives easier or to get ahead. Procrastination does the opposite. It causes more trouble in the end and makes life very uncomfortable.

   Second, procrastination hurts others' perception of you. As you get older, more people will rely on you and expect specific things from you. Procrastination makes you appear lazy and unfocused to those watching you.

5. *Recognize your real priorities.* Stop reading for a second and take out a pen and paper. Jot down the top three priorities in your life. You probably listed one or more of the following: God, friends, family, work, church, school, a sport, yourself, or a significant other. If someone followed you around for one day, would how you spend your time prove to that person that these things are your priorities? For most people, there is a big gap between what they think their priorities are and what their lives show their priorities to be. Think about what you did yesterday. Based on the way you spent your time, what would someone say is a priority for you?

   Listed on the next page are some important priorites. Beside each are tips to help you make them your true priorities:

- Your relationship with God – Spend 20 minutes each day in Bible study and prayer.
- Church – Serve somewhere in your church every week.
- Friends – Spend one-to-one time with a friend each week.
- Family – Eat dinner with your family at least twice a week. If you won't live at home after graduation, make a point of spending a lot of quality time with them when you visit. (Translation: Don't come home for the weekend and spend the whole time away from your family.)
- God – Spend some time reading a book that teaches you about His attributes.

For most people, there is a big gap between what they think their priorities are and what their lives show their priorities to be.

For Me Or for God?

Jesus provided a framework for making the most of every second, minute, hour, day, and year of your life. He said in Matthew 6:33-34, "Seek first the kingdom of God and His righteousness, and all these things will be provided for you. Therefore don't worry about tomorrow, because tomorrow will worry about itself. Each day has enough trouble of its own."

There is a difference between making the most of every hour for yourself and making the most of every hour for God. How can you make time count for God?

1. *See life as God sees it.* See people as God sees them. See time as God sees time—as something to use wisely. Be sensitive to God at all times. You may discover new ways to make life count.
2. *Realize life is not about you.* It is about God. It is not about your rights and wishes. It is about God's glory.
3. *Focus on your relationship with God instead of activity for God.* Don't confuse busyness for God with a relationship with Him. Be intentional about relating intimately with God.
4. *Ask God to change your schedule as He sees fit.* When He changes your plans, get ready. God wants to use you!

5. *Ask God to change your future plans.* My plan in high school and college was to be an accountant. I am now a full-time minister. Allowing God to change your plans does not always mean He will lead you to be a pastor. The point is to be sensitive to the ways God leads you and to be obedient to Him.

Focus on your relationship with God instead of activity for God. Don't confuse busyness for God with a relationship with Him.

Extra Credit

- Read *Tyranny of the Urgent* and *Freedom from Tyranny of the Urgent* by Charles E. Hummel to discover more about priorities and wise time management.
- Check out the resources in the "Time Management" section of the CD-ROM. They can help you make the most of the time God has given you.
- Spend time meditating on Psalm 39:4-5 and James 4:14. Write in your journal your thoughts on the shortness of life and how it motivates you to live differently.
- Spend some time alone—away from noise, people, distractions—and read 1 Peter 5:7 and Matthew 11:28 several times. Give God your stresses and burdens. Allow Him to change the way you feel about these things. Spend time quietly resting with Jesus.
- Read Exodus 18:13-24 to see how Moses modeled how to drop things that cause extreme stress.

1. Mike Fernandez, "Get Me To My Life On Time," *Christian Single*, June 2002: 44-45.

The glory of friendship is ... the spiritual inspiration that comes to one when he discovers that someone else believes in him and is willing to trust him with his friendship.
—Ralph Waldo Emerson

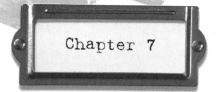

Chapter 7

DON'T GO IT ALONE

T he things our friends can talk us into doing! Recently I was at a large amusement park walking around with a group of my friends. We came upon a ride that looked like a cross between a human slingshot, skydiving, and a Superman flight simulator. It was called the Xtreme Skyflyer™. It was exactly the kind of ride I had never tried for a million reasons. Reason number one: I don't like heights. Reason number two: There had to be some way to fall out of that harness. Reasons three through a million: I always thought it was best to leave flying to birds, airplanes, and superheroes.

We plummeted straight down toward the ground, and then we flew forward and then backward through the air like Superman going 100 miles per hour! (Well, it felt that fast.)

So did I take on their dare? Of course I did! My friends prodded me on. Out of the eight of us, only two of us actually tried out the contraption. My friend Daniel and I were pulled back and lifted up 10 miles off the ground (well, it seemed that high); all we could do was stare straight down at the scenery below. We couldn't move any part of our bodies since we were strapped into that harness. After a very quick "3-2-1," the cord that pulled us up suddenly released us. We plummeted straight down toward the ground, and then we flew forward and then backward through the air like Superman going 100 miles per hour! (Well, it felt that fast.)

I have to admit something—it was awesome! It was one of the scariest and most fun things I've ever done! I'm so glad my friends prodded me on to do it. (But I'll never do it again!)

Isn't It Ironic?

Everyone wants friends. Even the most shy or most independent individuals want people around with whom they can share life. But many people give the impression that they don't really need anybody else—that they can't count on anybody else.

The truth is we are relational beings. We need people. God wired us this way. He made us in His image, and He is relational.

The truth is we are relational beings. We need people. God wired us this way. He made us in His image, and He is relational. But there is a part of each of us that wants to think the only person we truly need is ourself. That is a lie.

Check out what the Bible says about friendship: "Two are better than one because they have a good reward for their efforts. For if either falls, his companion can lift him up; but pity the one who falls without another to lift him up. Also, if two lie down together, they can keep warm; but how can one person alone keep warm?" (Eccl. 4:9-11).

No Better Way to Say It

"Two are better than one." There is no better way for God to tell us that we need other people in our lives. He could cause every person to be born connected to another person like conjoined brothers or sisters who do everything and go everywhere together. That could classify as a relationship. But God didn't create us like that. He does not force us to have friendships. He does tell us, though, that we need friends. It is up to us to decide what we're going to do with what He tells us.

Friends are essential to your life! Why? Look back at Ecclesiastes 4:9-11. First, a friend can help you accomplish more than you can accomplish by yourself. It's called synergy. Basically, *synergy* means 1+1=3. The sum or the result is greater than individual parts. For example, David can produce 5 gadgets. Stephanie can produce 7 gadgets. When David and Stephanie work together, though, they can produce 15 gadgets. When they work together they can produce more. This is the power of friendship—two people working in agreement. No doubt, you can have results if you go it alone. But imagine what you can do when you partner with a friend.

5 7

It is reassuring to have a friend who knows you well enough to come alongside when you need it, even when you can't express what you're feeling.

Second, a friend can pick you up when you fall. You may suffer from a broken heart, hurt feelings, a physical problem, a spiritual battle, or any number of life's circumstances. Life will knock you down. Of course, you can pick yourself up on your own. It is a lonely feeling, though, when you are down and look around and there is no one around to help you up. It is reassuring to have a friend who knows you well enough to come alongside when you need it, even when you can't express what you're feeling.

Your friendships determine the direction and quality of your life.

Under the Influence

Life is full of cause-and-effect relationships. If you don't brush your teeth, you will get cavities (and no one will want to hang around you very long!). If you never put gas in your car, your car will stop running. If you drink a gallon of water, you will have to go to the rest room—often. If you have a friend, he or she will influence you. Friendship equals influence, so establishing and maintaining good friendships is vital. Proverbs 13:20 advises, "The one who walks with the wise will become wise, but a companion of fools will suffer harm." If you have wise friends, you will become wise. If you have foolish friends, you will become a fool.

I keep a picture from my wedding close to my computer. In the picture, my wife is surrounded by my groomsmen. At the time, they were eight friends with whom I spent most of my time. Today, four of them are doctors, two are pastors, one is a parachurch ministry leader, and one is a fireman. They are Christians serving other people in the area in which God has called them to serve. I did not think about it at the time, but I was walking with the wise. They were influencing me in ways I did not realize.

If you have wise friends, you will become wise. If you have foolish friends, you will become a fool.

Another story paints a different picture: Tonya was a smart girl. She was the first in her family to go to college. She had never really had a boyfriend, so when Doug showed an interest in her, she jumped into a relationship with him immediately. She dropped out of college to marry him and have his child. They had been married for only a few years when Doug became involved with someone else. They divorced around the time Tonya would have graduated from college. Tonya's life was severely altered because she became the companion of a fool.

A true friend will love you regardless of the circumstances or situation. The commitment to the friendship may be tested, but it is never broken.

What a Friend Looks Like

Wise, healthy, true friendships have certain characteristics. Regardless of your age, personality, or interests, the kind of friendships you need are marked by several key qualities.

1. *Unconditional love.* Proverbs 17:17 states, "A friend loves at all times." Unconditional love states, "I love you no matter what." A true friend will love you regardless of the circumstances or situation. The commitment to the friendship may be tested, but it is never broken. Unconditional love

does not mean that you will always agree with someone else or that you approve of his actions. It does mean, however, that you're committed to remain friends.

Unconditional love does not mean that you will always agree with someone else or that you approve of his actions.

2. *Faithfulness*. Proverbs 18:24 says, "A man with many friends may be harmed, but there is a friend who stays closer than a brother." A true friend is your friend in the good times and *especially* the bad times. This proverb defines a faithful friend as someone who sticks with you more than your own family member. You never have to worry about this friend's loyalty to you.

3. *Accountability*. Proverbs 27:17 says, "Iron sharpens iron, and one man sharpens another." Iron sharpens iron to make both metals stronger and more useful. A good friend will hold you accountable for your actions (tell you when you're being stupid or acting like a jerk) and challenge you to become a person who's stronger, better, and more useful for God. A good friend will not always agree with you or approve of what you are doing. A true friend asks tough questions and has high expectations for who you should be.

A good friend will not always agree with you or approve of what you are doing.

What About . . . ?
Friendships are great, but they can be a little tough sometimes. As you mature, you're likely to face some challenges in your friendships. Let's look at three of these issues.

1. *What about non-Christian and Christian friendships?* Every Christian should develop friendships with non-Christians, but a Christian's closest friends should be followers of Christ. Why? Think of the examples

you read about earlier. If a Christian is too closely connected to a non-Christian, there is a real danger in the non-Christian drawing the Christian away from God. God gives a strong warning concerning this in 2 Corinthians 6:14-18. In every relationship, influence will happen. The Christian must be wise about which way the influence is happening.

Every Christian should develop friendships with non-Christians, but a Christian's closest friends should be followers of Christ.

2. *What about when friends go bad?* You will have friends who make poor choices or do things they should not do. You may even need to spend some time apart because they're involved in things you need to stay away from. What should you do when this happens?
   - Pray for them. Pray specifically for their actions.
   - Make sure you don't support their poor choices.
   - Show them unconditional love—even when you disagree.
   - Do not gossip about them.
   - Confront them about their actions in a loving way.
   - Be willing to help them get going in the right direction. (In other words, don't completely disown them!)
   - Show them the consequences of their poor choices.
   - If necessary, end the friendships by telling them this is the only way left for you to show them love.

You may even need to spend some time apart because they're involved in things you need to stay away from.

3. *What about when friends grow apart?* Some friendships, even strong friendships, will fade over time. The friends you have now probably will not be your friends five years from now. Changes in friendships are a natural part of growing up. Why? A number of factors contribute to fading friendships.

- Distance. Friendships grow when you invest time into them. When distance becomes a factor, friends cannot spend as much time together.
- Different interests. After high school, you and your friends will have more freedom to pursue interests you've never been exposed to before. Those who go on to college pursue a field of study. Those who work pursue work-related goals. Common interests bring people together; different interests can sometimes send people apart.
- Different maturity levels. As people gain more independence and responsibilities after high school, they mature at different rates. A person typically wants to have friends who have a similar maturity level.
- New friendships. New friendships usually replace old friendships for all of the reasons mentioned above.

The great thing about friendships is that while some friendships fade, others blossom. You are created as a relational being, and God will provide some amazing friends along the way.

Extra Credit
- Read about the following friendships in the Bible: Jonathan and David in 1 Samuel 13-23 and 2 Samuel 1; Jesus and His disciples in Matthew, Mark, Luke, and John; and Paul and the many friends he wrote about in his letters.
- Use a Web site like *www.lifeway.com/bible* to do a word search on the word *friend*. As you read each verse, ask yourself questions like: *What does this verse teach me about friendship? What is God saying about friendships? How can I become a better friend because of this verse?*
- Check out the section, "Relationships" on the CD-ROM. You'll find Web sites, articles, and quizzes dealing with friendships and other relationships.

1. Andy Stanley and Stuart Hall, *The Seven Checkpoints For Youth Leaders* (West Monroe, Louisiana: Howard Publishing Co., Inc., 2001), 101.

More men fail through lack of purpose
than through lack of talent.
—W.A. "Billy" Sunday

CREATED WITH PURPOSE

W hat does the future hold for you? For some of you, the future is an open book. You will be moving into dorms and apartments with roommates, you will be starting new jobs, you will be encountering new friends. It is an amazing time in your life, but where does God come into play in that future? What kind of purpose does He have for your life? The answer will either amaze you or scare you. Read the story of the Israelites to learn about God's plan for you.

A Lesson from History Class

To understand the idea of God having a plan and a purpose for your life, we need to go back to the year 605 B.C. The armies of King Nebuchadnezzar of Babylon had taken over Jerusalem. Nebuchadnezzar gave orders to collect the best and the brightest young Israelites—including Daniel, Hananiah, Mishael, and Azariah—and take them back to Babylon. You may know the last three by the names given to them by their captors—Shadrach, Meshach, and Abednego. These young Israelite men were in the prime of their lives, but they must have felt lost, abandoned, and afraid as they walked through the desert on their way to Babylon. What was their purpose now that they'd been sentenced to live in a foreign country? Had God abandoned His chosen people?

A Message of Hope

Fast-forward 20 years. A man named Jeremiah sent a letter that was a message from God. Written to the Jews still living in Babylon after all this time, the letter encouraged the Jewish exiles to be productive in Babylon—build houses, marry, have kids, start careers. In other words, God was telling His chosen people to make themselves at home in this land of exile and captivity away from all they had ever known. This was not what the people wanted to hear. The God who told them He would never forsake them wrote them a letter to tell them that He had no plans to rescue them anytime soon. The letter concluded with a message of hope, but it was preceded by the disappointing timetable—God would restore them and bring them back home—in 70 years! (See Jer. 29:11.)

How can God say He has a plan for my life when I have just been told that I will die in this land of captivity? How can God say He is giving me a hope and a future when all I have to look forward to is the day of my death?

Put yourself in the sandals of an exiled Jewish teenager living in Babylon. You've been hanging onto the hope that things would change and you would be delivered from captivity, but you've just been told that you will spend your life in captivity. Then to further confuse the situation, Jeremiah revealed a great promise of God. He said, "For I know the plans I have for you, . . . plans for your welfare, not for disaster, to give you a future and a hope" (Jer. 29:11). You might think, *Future? Hope? How can God say He has a plan for my life when I have just been told that I will die in this land of captivity? How can God say He is giving me a hope and a future when all I have to look forward to is the day of my death?*

God was indeed faithful to keep His promises, but according to His will, timetable, and plan—not according to the Jewish people's plan.

The End of the Story

So how does the story end? Exactly 70 years later, the Jews were given their release from captivity. God was indeed faithful to keep His promises, but according to His will, timetable, and plan—not according to the Jewish people's plan. In the big scheme of things, the Jewish people gained a more God-centered perspective on the purpose for their lives.

Through the plan of God, humanity was brought back into a relationship with God. It is that act that gives each believer a purpose in life.

The Grand Scheme

Eventually the people were led back to Jerusalem, and eventually, a child was born to a descendant of one of the exiles. That child was named Jesus. On a Roman cross, He gave the Jewish people the certain hope and the permanent future they had been promised 600 years earlier in the letter from Jeremiah—Jesus gave them eternal deliverance from their sins.

"I don't care if I get a PhD or clean parking lots as long as people see God in my life." —Ben, age 21

Although the companionship between God and humanity had been severed in a garden, the plan of God was to open the door for reconciliation through the amazing work of Jesus Christ on the cross. And because that work was done, you have been given a great purpose and plan for your life. But be prepared—it's not about marriage, family, career, adventure, or success. It's much bigger than that. The ultimate plan and purpose for you is to live a life of trust and obedience to Jesus in response to His extravagant demonstration of love toward you on that cross. Your future should not be evaluated solely by whether you go to school, meet the right person, or find the perfect job. These things need to be seen as tools for fulfilling the greatest purpose in your life—to pursue a life of passion and worship directed at the One who gave His life for You.

The ultimate purpose for you is to live a life of trust and obedience to Jesus in response to His extravagant demonstration of love toward you on that cross.

Live or Die? Yes!

The Apostle Paul gave a great challenge in Romans 12:1-2. He told the Christians in Rome that they ought to present themselves as "living sacrifices." The motivation for this ironic way of life was in response to the mercy of God given through Christ on the cross. So how does that play out in everyday life? A living sacrifice is concerned that his career allows him to honor God. A living sacrifice is concerned with getting married only if that relationship allows her to fulfill her primary purpose of loving and serving Jesus. True followers of Christ will always pursue God's glory over their own; people who just show up for church never even consider it. The purpose for our lives is to cease our pursuit of individual greatness and to live for the honor of the One who showed us such incredible mercy.

"Therefore, brothers, by the mercies of God, I urge you to present your bodies as a living sacrifice, holy and pleasing to God; this is your spiritual worship. Do not be conformed to this age, but be transformed by the renewing of your mind, so that you may discern what is the good, pleasing, and perfect will of God."
—Romans 12:1-2

While the rest of the world sets its mind on success, wealth, and health, the believer sets his mind on fulfilling God's purpose for him—which redefines success, wealth, and health. Followers of Jesus live with a sweet discomfort in this life as they strive for the eternal things of another world.

Living Sacrifices Ought to Live

Does this mean we all need to crawl into a bunker and just pray all the time, sing praise choruses, and go on mission trips to foreign countries? Not at all! In fact, fulfilling your purpose in the world is where your future lies. Your task is not to remove yourself from the world but to be a bright light in a very dark world, whether you go to college, go into the workforce immediately, or choose to serve your country through military service. God wants to use you in your arena of influence as you engage your world.

God wants to use those very unique and valuable talents and passions to honor Him and draw others to know His love and mercy like you do.

Let's illustrate this with a story: A Christian college student was torn between reading history textbooks (he was going to school to become a history teacher) or spending more time studying his Bible. A wise man asked him this question: which would be more honoring to God—to be an average teacher or to be an excellent teacher? The wise man was trying to help the college student understand that what we do on a daily basis should fulfill our calling to honor God with our entire lives—whether that be studying, sacking groceries, being a medic in the marine corps, or just taking your car to the shop for repair. Obviously, those pursuits should not hinder your daily walk with God—prayer, Bible study, worship. Your passionate pursuit of God should impact every area of your life.

What we do on a daily basis should fulfill our calling to honor God with our entire lives—whether that be studying, sacking groceries, being a medic in the marine corps, or taking your car to the shop for repair.

So if we're all called to a future of love and worship toward God, what about our own individuality and unique giftedness? Where do you find your future? King David wrote in Psalm 139 that the days of your life were written out before you were even born. Does that mean you do not have control over your choices, that God has already written the script and you are merely reading lines? No. It means that your life is not a random collection of events and interests. Your interest in music is not some disconnected passion. Your ability in English is not a genetic accident. God wants to use those very unique and valuable talents and passions to honor Him and draw others to know His love and mercy like you do. We are gifted and are passionate about different things because God is calling us to fulfill our purpose through these things.

Use Your Passion for His Glory

So what does that mean for your future? It may be that your passion to help people will lead you to a career or ministry focusing on homelessness, AIDS, or adoption. Your ability to hit a baseball 400 feet will lead you to play professional baseball for the honor of your Savior. The little restaurant you always wanted to open may become a national chain of restaurants. Wherever your gifts and abilities meet with God's direction, be careful not to evaluate your future according to dollar signs and comfort level. You will feel fulfilled only when your purpose meshes with bringing God glory, because that is what you were created to do.

Who's Your Daddy?

What do you do if you cannot find your place in this world? First, do not look for purpose in the world's definition of value. The things the world considers important are not what the Bible teaches to be valuable.

Second, remember that your future is guided by a God whose throne is accessible. If you need direction, just ask and then listen. If you need clarification, ask and listen. The Bible is clear that God is not an aloof God who vindictively leaves you to find your way alone. He desires to lead you into the place in life that will bring Him honor and bring you fulfillment.

In the Sermon on the Mount, Jesus told His listeners that they needed only to ask for things from God in order to receive them. Jesus explained that His followers do not have a God who would ever trick or harm them. Instead, just like a loving father, your Heavenly Father wants the very best for your life. And your best interests are served by your reliance and trust in Him. (See Matt. 7:7-12.)

How will you define your purpose in life? Will it be the value of money? Security and comfort? Relationships? Worldly success? Or will the exclamation of your life point others to the cross, where they will see the Savior you love and worship?

The Defining Purpose

How will you define your purpose in life? Will it be the value of money? Security and comfort? Relationships? Worldly success? Or will the exclamation of your life point others to the cross, where they will see the Savior you love and worship? As you consider your future, establish Christ as the defining purpose for every breath you take and every beat of your heart. In line with that mind-set, consider the ways in which God has given you abilities and passions. Then begin to process how you can use those passions and gifts for the glory of God's kingdom. Seek the guidance of God with all your heart. You'll find your purpose in those moments.

Extra Credit

- Study Matthew 6:25-34. What does this say about the way your life is working out? Practice applying this principle to at least one area of your life and see what God will do.
- Make a list of things you are really passionate about and allow God to use those over the next five years to define His plans for your life. Based on your passions, what is the wildest life you could possibly imagine? Dream big! And pray that God would do big things.

Occupation was one of the
pleasures of Paradise, and we
cannot be happy without it.
—Anna Jameson

Chapter 9

ON THE JOB

Now that you're graduating from high school, what will you do with the rest of your life? Unless you are independently wealthy, you'll need to get a job doing something. Have you thought about what kind of job you want to have? Maybe you'd like to become a vermiculturist. A what? That's fancy terminology for a worm farmer. Maybe you like working outside, but not in the dirt. Then being a storm chaser might be more up your alley. These folks do just that—they chase bad storms to learn about weather systems (just like in the movie *Twister*).

You could be a roller coaster designer, a food stylist, a demolitionist, a lighthouse operator, a pet-sitter, an ostrich farmer, a butterfly feeder, a Wall Street investor, a teacher, a lawyer, a test pilot, a wind turbine mechanic, or even an archeologist.

OK, so maybe you grew up around tornadoes and you're phobic of storms. Then your options are still wide open. You could be a roller coaster designer (be prepared to spend lots of time in front of a computer), a food stylist (they arrange and style foods used in ads, movies, and TV commercials), or a matador (only if you're quick on your feet). You could be a demolitionist, a ethnomusicologist (I'll let you look that one up in the dictionary), a lighthouse operator, a pet-sitter, an ostrich farmer, a butterfly feeder, a Wall Street investor, a teacher, a lawyer, a test pilot, a wind turbine mechanic, or even an archeologist (back to digging in the dirt). What if you still can't decide what you want to do? Then try being a vocational evaluator. These folks administer tests to people who want to change careers, then counsel them on finding a new line of work.

How you feel about the work you do could be the difference between a life of frustration and a life of impact.

Whether you like it or not, you will spend much of your life in some type of job doing some type of work. So how will you honor God and bring glory to Him while on the job? Well, it mostly depends on your outlook on your job—the lenses through which you view your career. Your view of work will make a tremendous difference in your life and in the lives of those around you. How you feel about the work you do could be the difference between a life of frustration and a life of impact.

Why Work?
Wouldn't life be great if we didn't have to work? Wouldn't it be wonderful if all we had to do was pursue our passions and hobbies, spend time with friends, go to the beach, hang out at the house, and enjoy life? Such a life may not be as terrific as it sounds. Let's find out why.

God established work before sin entered the world. Work is not a punishment or a consequence of sin. Work is good. We are created to work!

The fall of humanity is recorded in Genesis 3. You're familiar with the story—the serpent's temptation and Adam and Eve's fatal sin that affected all of us. Things got bad after that. But everything before Genesis 3 was incredible! Humanity's relationship with God was intimate and very real.

Adam and Eve literally communicated back and forth with God. They related to each other openly and without shame. There was peace. Life was beautiful. And guess what? Even before sin entered the picture, they worked. Check out this verse:

"The Lord God took the man and placed him in the garden of Eden to work it and watch over it" (Gen. 2:15).

Did you catch that? God established work before sin entered the world. Work is not a punishment or a consequence of sin. Work is good. We are created to work!

Why Do You Work?

God wants you to work. When He created you, He created you to work. Within the human soul is the need to be productive, to be creative, to have satisfaction and fulfillment from a "job well done." The problem is that most people pursue the wrong career because their focus is in the wrong place.

What motivates you to work? The number one motivation for people to work is money, regardless of whether they are a Christian or not. People need money so they can provide for their basic needs, do what they want to do, and accumulate the things they want to accumulate. And the primary way to get money is to work. But is the motivation of money enough to provide satisfaction and contentment?

"Take Robert, an executive in Cincinnati who took a job for great money—more than $200,000—but is chucking it all. 'I make a lot of money, but I have no life. . . . I have no time for relationships and little control over my time. I'm not even that thrilled with the job. I'm more miserable now than before I was making good money. What's the point?' "[1]

Robert's realization about the motivation of money is echoed in Ecclesiastes 5:10. Solomon said, "The one who loves money is never satisfied with money, and whoever loves wealth is never satisfied with income. This too is futile." If you work for money, you will never be satisfied. Robert had a job that paid more than most people will ever earn, and it made him miserable.

Another motivation people have for pursuing a job is pride. They want to feel superior. Through work, they feel important and needed. And with pride comes a sense of power. Pride is a dangerous trap, though. "In his pride the wicked does not seek him; in all his thoughts there is no room for God" (Ps. 10:4, NIV). Pride causes people to focus on themselves. All of the attention and all of the credit goes to them. There is no room and no need for God. He has been replaced on the throne by them. The consequence of pride is clearly stated in Proverbs 11:2, "When pride comes, disgrace follows, but with humility comes wisdom." Pride may give a brief fulfillment, but shame and embarrassment will follow eventually.

Christians work because God created us to work, and work is good. We work to bring God glory. We work to represent Him to the world.

Whether you make tacos at a fast-food restaurant, manage a bank, cut lawns, or work in retail, you do not work for a person or a company. You do not work for your customers. Regardless of the type of job you have, you work for God.

Who's Your Boss?

Whether you make tacos at a fast-food restaurant, manage a bank, cut lawns, or work in retail, you do not work for a person or a company. You do not work for your customers. Regardless of the type of job you have, you work for God. Colossians 3:22-24 states, "Slaves, obey your human masters in everything; don't work only while being watched, in order to please men, but work wholeheartedly, fearing the Lord. Whatever you do, do it enthusiastically, as something done for the Lord and not for men, knowing that you will receive the reward of an inheritance from the Lord—you serve the Lord Christ."

Wow. Do you realize the power of these verses? When we work, we're ultimately working for God. That means we offer our best, even when the job isn't the most glamorous or exciting. What does it mean to work as unto God? In practical terms, how you behave on the job should be a reflection of your relationship with God. In the last chapter, you learned that your purpose was to honor God and draw people to Him. In practical terms, how do you demonstrate your faith and character at work?

First, treat your boss with respect, even if you're treated poorly. Every time you work, you are representing God to your boss. Paul made sure to write that we are to obey our bosses. Our attitudes should never be, "I work for God and not you!" Our attitudes should be, "I serve God by the way I work for you." How you treat your boss is a reflection of your relationship with Christ.

Second, demonstrate diligence in your work even when no one is looking. Many people slack off when no one is watching. You should be diligent in your work even when the boss, coworkers, or customers are not watching you. If you only work hard when someone is watching, you are working to please people. You may be pleasing people, but you are not pleasing God, who is your ultimate boss. God sees what you do, and He wants to take pleasure in how you are representing Him regardless of who your audience is.

True character is measured by what you do when nobody is looking.

Third, maintain the right kind of attitude. Everything we do should be done with an attitude of servanthood and service, as if everything we do is for God and not people. Our audience is an audience of one: God. Picture yourself at work. Now picture yourself working for God. How would your work habits change if you really worked as if you were working for your Savior?

Fourth, stay faithful. Faithfulness in your work will get people's attention because most workers simply do not demonstrate this quality. Faithfulness means your work is not about you; it is about God and other people. When you don't get a raise, when you are overlooked for the promotion, when you don't get the better schedule, when things don't go your way, you do not quit. That is faithfulness.

When you don't get a raise, when you are overlooked for the promotion, when you don't get the better schedule, you do not quit. That is faithfulness.

When you respond in a godly way even in a bad circumstance, it becomes obvious to those watching that something is different about you. Of course, this does not mean staying in a job in which you are being taken advantage of. But it does mean working where God wants you to work regardless of whether or not things always go the way you want.

Working for Others

Let's face it, Christians have given themselves a bad name, especially in the workplace. Some Christians lie, steal, act lazy, gossip, disrespect their bosses—the list could go on. You may be thinking, *Wait a minute. People who are not Christians do the same things at their jobs.* You're right, but Christians are supposed to be different. We represent God to the world.

Christians have given themselves a bad name, especially in the workplace. Some Christians lie, steal, act lazy, gossip, disrespect their bosses—the list could go on.

First Thessalonians 4:11-12 instructs, "Seek to lead a quiet life, to mind your own business, and to work with your own hands, as we commanded you, so that you may walk properly in the presence of outsiders and not be dependent on anyone." These verses tell you how to work honorably.

1. Lead a life that does not draw attention to yourself. Work quietly within the standards and convictions you have determined for yourself. Decide what you are not willing to do: lie, cheat, steal, gossip, or disrespect your boss. Decide this before you are put in situations in which you are tempted to do these things; then never allow yourself to compromise your standards, even when those around you compromise theirs.

2. Do not get caught up in petty games with people. Serve people. Help people. Do not play emotional or social games with people. Don't gossip or talk about coworkers or your supervisors. Treat others with respect. Treat others as significant.

3. Be purposeful about working. Make sure you work when you are at work. Do not allow yourself to act or appear lazy. Making time for relaxing and resting is vital to your health, but work time is not the time for hanging out, chilling out, or goofing off. If you really want others to notice a difference in your life because you're a believer, then do things without asking. Perform menial tasks that other coworkers would consider "beneath them" (like cleaning the bathrooms). Go beyond what your job description requires if the work needs to be done.

What will happen if you do these three things consistently? Your life will be noticed by others because it is so different. You will win the respect of non-Christians and create interest in knowing this Jesus we serve.

Making time for relaxing and resting is vital to your health, but work time is not the time for hanging out, chilling out, or goofing off.

Our Model
The biblical character Daniel modeled this type of work life and lifestyle. Daniel 6:3-4 reads, "Daniel distinguished himself above the administrators and satraps [governors in the Persian Empire] because he had an extraordinary spirit, so the king planned to set him over the whole realm. The administrators and satraps, therefore, kept trying to find a charge against Daniel regarding the kingdom. But they could find no charge or corruption, for he was trustworthy, and no negligence or corruption was found in him." Over and over, Daniel's priority was to honor God whether he was dealing with his boss or coworkers. Whether he was faced with prosperity, death, or a room full of wild animals, Daniel worked faithfully and caused others to pay attention to God. In the end, Daniel caused the king to create a new law requiring all people to worship God! (See Dan. 6:25-27.) Talk about working for God!

Extra Credit
- Read Daniel 1–6 and study how Daniel worked faithfully and saw his work as a calling from God. Look for ways to model Daniel's actions and attitudes at your work.
- Read *Keeping Your Head Up When Your Job's Got You Down* by Doug Sherman.
- Check out the "Job and Career" section of the CD-ROM for helpful articles, tips, and Web sites related to job and career issues.

1. Andrea Kay, "Be sure job offers more than money," *The Greenville News,*
   31 October 2004, F1.

Fools can make money.
It takes a wise man to tell how
to spend it. —English Proverb

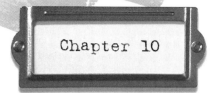

Chapter 10

SPENDING GOD'S MONEY

9

Imagine for a moment you've been given the opportunity to bungee jump off a cliff on some exotic island. You're standing in line behind other graduating seniors. You see them strap on the cord, receive instructions from seasoned guides, and make a flying leap over the edge. As you see the exhilaration on their faces, you wonder whether they are smiling from sheer joy or if they're trying to keep from throwing up. Your turn is quickly approaching; you must make a decision. You imagine two little men, one on each shoulder, debating the jump.

"Are you crazy? What if you get hurt?" screams one side.

The other replies, "Go for it! You just need to have a little trust. You're a big coward if you don't do it."

As the debate in your mind continues, you walk closer to the edge and look over a wide canyon of unknowns. With your gear in place and instructions in your head, you take one final look back and hear the countdown, "5 . . . 4 . . . 3 . . . 2 . . . 1 . . . Jump!"

Trusting God

Graduation is like taking a grand bungee jump into life. You face countless unknowns and millions of decisions. At times, you will experience sheer joy and at times, you will feel nauseated. You're learning to trust God in a lot of areas—including your finances.

Trusting God in your finances is a process you'll learn throughout your entire life. Whether or not you think you are ready to make decisions regarding money matters, it's an issue you can't avoid. In fact, it's such an important issue that the Bible contains more verses about money and stewardship than verses on heaven and hell.

In Matthew 6:24, Jesus said, "No one can be a slave of two masters, since either he will hate one and love the other, or be devoted to one and despise the other. You cannot be slaves of God and of money." Rick Warren explains this verse in his book *The Purpose Driven Life:* "When Jesus is your Master, money serves you, but if money is your master, you become its slave. Wealth is certainly not a sin, but failing to use it for God's glory is. Servants of God are always more concerned about ministry than money."[1]

One of the things you must come to grips with is simply this: how will you approach money—as a tool or as an idol?

The Bible contains more verses about money and stewardship than verses on heaven and hell.

God Owns It All

Psalm 24:1 says, "The earth and everything in it, the world and its inhabitants, belong to the LORD." In other words, everything you think is yours really isn't! Why does God own everything? Because He created everything. But even though God created everything, He allows humans the responsibility of managing creation. Even in the first chapter of the Bible, God said people would be given the job of ruling over creation. Ruling creation didn't mean misusing or exploiting it. God's call to us is to be good managers of creation. Our job is to do something positive with the resources entrusted to us.

You have been trusted with God's resources, and in turn, God will hold you accountable for the way you manage them.

So what's a steward? Historically, stewardship was a means to protect a kingdom while the king was away. The stewards were responsible for taking care of the king's property, resources, and money. God is our ultimate authority, or King, and He has given us the responsibility of caring for His creation. A steward is held accountable for his actions. You have been trusted with God's resources, and in turn, God will hold you accountable for the way you manage them. So what does that mean for you?

Giving Back to God First

You may not be in the habit of giving your high school teachers gifts, but do you remember bringing a gift to an elementary school teacher? Maybe it was for a special holiday (like Christmas), because you liked your teacher, or because your mom made you take it to her. Whatever the motivation, the gift was a token of appreciation for the investment your teacher made in your life.

As a believer, you have the same opportunity to express appreciation to God with a gift. Your expressions of love and trust could be your talents or your time given in service. But one of the ways God commands you to honor Him is with your finances—through a tithe.

If you've been in church much, you're probably familiar with the word *tithe*. Maybe your parents gave you money as a child to put in the church offering or they taught you about it at home. If you didn't grow up around church, the word *tithe* may sound totally foreign to you. So what is a tithe and why is it important?

God wants the first of your income. He wants your gift to be set aside before you make any other plans to spend your income. In short, He wants to be your first priority, not your last.

The word *tithe* literally means "tenth." Back in the Old Testament when money was measured in animals and farming, God instructed the Israelites to give back to Him a tenth of their possessions or wealth. They didn't give their leftovers—animals with defects or fruit unfit to eat. They gave God the very best of their possessions. This was called the "first fruits." Proverbs 3:9 says, "Honor the LORD with your possessions and with the first produce of your entire harvest." In today's language, that means God wants the first of your income. He wants your gift to be set aside before you make any other plans to spend your income. In short, He wants to be your first priority, not your last.

Learning How to Give

To learn several different aspects of giving, think of the word *stewards* as an acrostic with each letter representing a principle for being generous with your finances.

S—Giving should be SYSTEMATIC and planned.

Whether you earn a little by baby-sitting or a lot at a part-time job, now is the time to begin the habit of giving on a consistent basis. If you begin the discipline of giving from the little you earn now, it will be easier when you are earning a larger income. As soon as you cash your paycheck, set aside your tithe, one tenth of your check. The next time you're in a worship service, give your gift to God. If you have a checking account, write out your tithe check *before* you pay any bills or take out money for anything else.

If you begin the discipline of giving from the little you earn now, it will be easier when you are earning a larger income.

In 1 Corinthians 16:2, Paul encouraged the Christians, "On the first day of the week, each of you is to set something aside and save to the extent that he prospers, so that no collections will need to be made when I come." Paul told believers to make a plan for giving—something everyone could do, no matter what level of income they received. Remember, God takes first place, not last.

T – Giving reflects spiritual TRUSTWORTHINESS.

Jesus told a lot of stories to make spiritual points. Many times He used stories that involved handling money or wealth. At the end of one of His parables Jesus said, "So if you have not been trustworthy in handling worldly wealth, who will trust you with true riches?" (Luke 16:11, NIV). In other words, why would God trust you with spiritual riches if you can't manage your own money?

A person's bank account is a picture of her priorities. What a person spends money on reflects what that person values, whether it's food, clothes, a car, or a relationship. Think for a moment about the top five things you've spent money on in the past month. Chances are, most of them reveal something about your spiritual walk with Christ.

What a person spends money on reflects what that person values, whether it's food, clothes, a car, or a relationship.

E—Giving is EXPRESSED by a thankful and cheerful attitude.

You've probably heard the verse "God loves a cheerful giver" (2 Cor. 9:7), but what does it mean? It means your expression of giving is a true reflection of a spiritual condition. Do you give only because "you're supposed to" or do you give with a grateful heart?

W—Giving is an act of WORSHIP.

Why is the offering plate passed during a church service? Because giving is actually a way you worship God. It may not feel as much like worship because you're not singing or reading Scripture. But worship is giving honor to God for who He is. Our giving is an expression of gratitude for who He is. And that is worship.

A – Giving is an APPROPRIATE response to a real need.

You will have the opportunity to be a financial blessing to someone who has a specific need. Whether you are able to write a check for $100, buy a bag of groceries, or even donate your car to someone in need, your gift meets the genuine needs of others. Look around your church and you'll likely find any number of needs you can help meet.

Our giving is an expression of gratitude for who He is. And that is worship.

R—Giving is a REFLECTION of faith in God's provision.
Your giving will be in direct correlation to your trust in God. The familiar story of the widow who gave everything she had in Mark 12:41-44 is a great example of someone who trusted God to meet all of her needs, both material and spiritual. Remember, God is faithful. You can trust that He will provide for you.

D—Giving is DIRECTED from a heart of love, not legalism.
God wants your giving to come from the overflow of your love for Him. God is not the bill collector who stands ready to knock you down when you don't pay up. God is your best friend. Just as you want to give good gifts to those you love, God wants the same attitude from you.

S—SACRIFICIAL giving results in SPIRITUAL blessings.
The motive for giving back to God and to His work is not so you can "get things" from Him. Giving does not come with a promise of material or wealth. But the Bible does say that God blesses faithful giving. Luke 6:38 reads, "Give, and it will be given to you; a good measure—pressed down, shaken together, and running over—will be poured into your lap. For with the measure you use, it will be measured back to you."

Talk to older Christians who have given faithfully for years, and they will have many stories of God's faithfulness. Most of them will probably tell you that when they gave at least 10 percent to God, He somehow made the other 90 percent go farther. Whether the car kept running longer or an unexpected gift came in the mail, those who are generous in giving have many testimonies that can only be attributed to God's blessings in their lives.

"I have learned to be content in whatever circumstances I am. I know both how to have a little, and I know how to have a lot. In any and all circumstances I have learned the secret of being content—whether well-fed or hungry, whether in abundance or in need." —Philippians 4:11-12

Keeping Perspective

Within the next few months you may be preparing to leave home. At some point, you'll need to get a job. When you begin working full time, will your career choice be based on money? While there's nothing wrong with desiring to make a good salary, keep a perspective that God holds you accountable for what you do with that money.

God also wants you to learn contentment with money. Paul learned a lot about contentment during his days of ministry. In Philippians 4:11-12, he wrote, "I have learned to be content in whatever circumstances I am. I know both how to have a little, and I know how to have a lot. In any and all circumstances I have learned the secret of being content—whether well-fed or hungry, whether in abundance or in need." The next few years may be the only time in your life when you can put all your possessions in your vehicle! Use this to your advantage, and live in the freedom you can experience when you learn to be content with what you have.

The next few years may be the only time in your life when you can put all your possessions in your vehicle!

Lastly, realize that it will take time for you to have the same material possessions as your parents. Just as it took them time to accumulate enough money to buy a house and the furnishings and to support children, it will take you time to afford some of the same luxuries. Despite the advertising to "buy now, pay later," wait to make purchases until you have saved the money to pay for them.

Make a Plan

Knowing the principles of giving is only part of money management. God is concerned about the 10 percent you give back to Him, but He's just as concerned with how you manage the other 90 percent. You'll need to develop discipline in three areas of money management: saving, spending, and borrowing.

"I started teaching piano lessons while I was in high school, and I saved half of everything I made. Now that I'm in college, the discipline of saving has helped me tremendously." —Claire, college freshman

1. *Saving money:* This may sound like an impossible thing to do as a young adult with no money, but it can be the best financial decision you make. Saving money early in life means more money later in life. You probably can't put large amounts of money into savings, but here's a good rule of thumb: 10 percent of your income goes to God first, and 10 percent of your income goes into savings. Then live off the rest. That way, when your car breaks down (and it eventually will), you'll have funds saved up to pay for repairs.

2. *Spending money:* It's easier to spend money than it is to save money. But spending wisely means having a plan—a budget. What you "want" will always exceed the amount of money you have. So start with the amount you make and begin subtracting known expenses. If this sounds difficult, start recording everything you spend each day for a month. You'll get a good idea of where your money is going. Learn how to balance a checkbook and do online banking. *Always* record your trips to the local automated teller machine (ATM). Use the "Weekly Budget" planner located on the CD-ROM to help you make a plan. Remember, having a budget isn't a punishment; it's a guideline that actually will give you some freedom.

"I never realized how much money I spent on eating out. It was so much more than I thought."
—Ryan, college junior

3. *Borrowing money:* Ask any student who has graduated from high school in the past few years and he will tell you he got bombarded weekly from financial institutions offering credit cards. The promise of "easy money" sounds exactly that: easy. But charge $50 for a new coat, $25 for a dinner with a friend, and $100 for a book in your college bookstore, and you'll be

greeted with a bill the following month for $175. The effects of borrowing can definitely lead you down a destructive path. Proverbs 22:7 says, "The rich rule over the poor, and the borrower is a slave to the lender."

College students are tempted to obtain numerous college loans. Many schools report that the average amount students owe in student loans when they graduate is approximately $14,000. Add an average of $2,750 credit card debt, and most students graduate owing a total of $16,750.[2] What took so little time to spend may take you years to pay back, along with the interest you will owe.

While some people argue that your earning power will be greater with a college degree, do your best to curb large student loans. Ask the Lord for wisdom and look for ways to obtain scholarships and other type of financial aid. See the CD-ROM for more information on financial aid Web sites and a "Financial Aid Vocabulary."

Jumping Safely

You wouldn't bungee jump without the bungee cord. That would be suicide. If you decide to take a financial leap without being connected to God's principles in money management, you can be headed for disaster. Don't leave high school without a good grasp on money management skills. Ask a lot of questions before you take the leap and be prepared for a lifetime.

Extra Credit

- Keep a notebook for a month and record every time you spend money. Make categories for food, clothes, entertainment, gas, and other regular expenses. This will help you evaluate your spending.
- Find someone in your church who has tithed for many years. Ask him to share some stories of how God blessed his commitment to giving.
- Search www.italladdsup.org and play some of the simulated games to learn principles about saving, buying a car, and much more.
- Use the "Budget Creator" located on the CD-ROM (under "Money Management") to help you make a spending plan. Remember, having a budget isn't a punishment; it's a guideline that will give you some freedom.

1. Rick Warren, *The Purpose Driven Life* (Grand Rapids, Mich.: Zondervan Publishing, 2002), 267.
2. "Collegiate Case Study: Money Matters for College Students," *USA Today* [online], [cited 17 Feb. 2005]. Available from Internet: www.usatodaycollege.com.

Attempt great things for God;
expect great things from God.
—William Carey

Chapter 11

WHERE DO YOU THINK YOU'RE GOING?

I t was the most desolate place I had ever been. Our church had driven one summer on a mission trip to a Navajo Indian reservation to conduct a Vacation Bible School. I didn't have a lot of responsibility that week until the VBS director asked me to lead the Bible study on the final day of our mission trip. We were working with Navajo adults as well as children. As a high school senior, I had never led a Bible study for adults, and I feared they had a greater knowledge of the Bible than I did. How could I, as a high school student, lead adults?

The evening before the Bible study, I asked God for direction and guidance. When it was all over, I hadn't told the most polished story of Nicodemus; but God was with me through my anxiety, and His story was heard. By the end of the week, my faith had been stretched. I discovered that faith in Jesus is not just something to be lived out on Sunday morning—it affects my life throughout the week.

My spiritual life experienced a growth spurt through the mission experience with the Navajo people. My view of the world around me was widened as I saw it—for the first time—through Christ's eyes. It was at that point in my spiritual walk that I made a pivotal decision in my life. After the prophet Isaiah had been in the presence of almighty God (Isa. 6:1-8), he said, "Here I am. Send me." After that trip to the Navajo reservation, I too made that decision. I didn't know what God had around the corner for me, but I made myself available for whatever He wanted.

Hopefully, you've had some mission experiences that have stretched your faith. As you graduate from high school, you'll encounter even more opportunities to grow spiritually—especially in the arenas of missions and evangelism. As a young adult, you have the potential to impact the world with the message of God's love.

Jesus' Expedition Orders

As He ascended into heaven, Jesus said, "Go, therefore, and make disciples of all nations, baptizing them in the name of the Father and of the Son and of the Holy Spirit, teaching them to observe everything I have commanded you. And remember, I am with you always, to the end of the age" (Matt. 28:19-20). Jesus didn't say, "Think about going to make disciples." He didn't say, "Go if no one else will." And He definitely didn't say, "Stay here and wait for people to find you." He commanded all of us to go and share good news wherever He leads. So what does that mean? Do you have to go to Africa? Do you have to give up your career plans? And what about the needs of people who live across the street? What is your role?

Jesus didn't say, "Think about going to make disciples." He didn't say, "Go if no one else will." And He definitely didn't say, "Stay here and wait for people to find you."

Let's look at the above verses we call the Great Commission. Look closely. What words within the Great Commission do you see as significant? Check out the word *them*. It's used twice. See the focus? It's all about people. The "thems"—people who need to know about a relationship with Jesus—are not only on the other side of the world; they're also in our own neighborhoods, classrooms, and workplaces.

How can you be "on course" in your mission efforts as a high school senior? You can be a missionary disguised as a student on your school campus. You don't have to look far to see needs of hurting students around you. They are evident in the words, actions, and attitudes of spiritually lost students. You can share Christ with people on the other side of the country (or around the world), and you can go across the hall at school and reach students you have known all your life. It may be tough and may seem impossible, but the same God who provided the strength, courage, and words while you were on a mission trip can help you reach your campus. You must first be "on mission" for Jesus where you are right now—at your school, in your home, at work, on your sports teams, in your community, and in your church.

Many students have found direction and purpose in life by developing a lifestyle of missions and service. For example, as a high school student, my brother Ron had an interest in flying and aviation. He learned that God could use his skills as a private pilot in aviation missions. When he graduated from high school, college, and then flight school, he served in South America flying medical emergencies in the most remote areas of Venezuela. His missions adventure began early in life at home, in the church, and at school. God cultivated that missions lifestyle into a career.

God may not call you to serve as a full-time missionary in some distant country (although He might)! He does want to use your gifts and abilities to serve Him and reach others. Think about your interests and passions, whether that be medicine, sports, or graphic design. God can use those gifts and abilities to share Jesus through lifestyle evangelism, short-term mission projects, and even career missions.

Be a missionary disguised as a student on your school campus!

Charting the Course

After Jesus' resurrection, He commanded His disciples to spread the good news everywhere they traveled. He said, "But you will receive power when the Holy Spirit has come upon you, and you will be My witnesses in Jerusalem, in all Judea and Samaria, and to the ends of the earth" (Acts 1:8). Let's take a look at each of these mission assignments a little closer.

1. *Jerusalem.* Jerusalem was close to home. The disciples probably bought and sold goods there. As Jews, they would travel there each year for religious ceremonies. Jerusalem was a part of their everyday lives.

So what is Jerusalem to you in the 21st century? Your Jerusalem can be your family and school—people you know and interact with on a regular basis. This can be the most difficult mission field because your family and classmates know you best. They notice when you're growing in your relationship with Christ, but they also know when you're rebelling against Him. Because this group of people knows you most intimately, the importance of living out the Christ-life is especially important.

2. *Judea.* Judea was an area of land between the Dead Sea and the Mediterranean Sea. It would be like a city, a region, or even a whole state. (Jerusalem was a part of Judea.) Notice the ripple effect of a missions mind-set. First, we reach out to those in our sphere of influence at home, at work, at school, and in our community. Then Jesus challenged His followers to reach out beyond the immediate sphere of influence—into Judea. For you, that may be others in the same town. It may be someone in a nearby town or another area of your state. While you may not have as frequent contact with people in this area, you can still be on mission to people in these regions. Maybe you're at a soccer tournament and stop at McDonald's®. Perhaps your youth group takes a trip across town to work at the soup kitchen. There are limitless opportunities. Just because you don't know these people as well does not relieve you of the responsibility of living out your faith in front of them.

Just because you don't know these people as well does not relieve you of the responsibility of living out your faith in front of them.

3. *Samaria.* The next area of concentration was an area north of Judah, like going to a different state. Jesus' command would have been difficult for the disciples to accept, because the Jews and Samaritans hated each other. Yet Jesus challenged people to go outside their comfort zones and love all people. For you this may mean going to a different state or area of the United States. Or it may mean reaching out to a different ethnic group or subculture on the college campus or military base.

4. *Ends of the earth.* Jesus told the disciples to go to the very ends of the earth in the task of making disciples. Many people would classify this as international missions. Jesus' challenge was simple but difficult—share

the good news everywhere, even on the other side of the world. This may take many forms: taking a short-term mission trip, going for a lifetime, or even serving for a couple of years. Whatever the length, God will bless it.

Chris Clayman, Journeyman (someone who does overseas missions for two years), told of a comment one person made to him. He wrote, "One person told me, 'You talk so much about love. Love your neighbor. Love God. All that is so hard for me to understand, because in my language, there is no word for love like you describe it.'"[1]

What things keep you from sharing Jesus with those in your Jerusalem? Your Judea? Your Samaria? Around the world? If you're honest, you'll admit that you're afraid. If that's the case, you need a good dose of courage. Remember, courage isn't the absence of fear. It's the willingness to act in spite of your fear.

Think about some people you don't want to go to heaven without. They are your motivation for sharing.

Faith and a Sense of Urgency

It's one thing to do something to fulfill an obligation. It's another thing to do something because you have a passion for it. In the same way, believers are to be passionate—even urgent—about sharing God with others. Why? Because of the eternal destination of those who reject Him. They're destined for an eternity without Him—a punishment too great to bear. Think about some people you don't want to go to heaven without. They are your motivation for sharing.

In the Book of Luke, Jesus used a figure of speech to communicate the need for a lifestyle of missions. He used the illustration of wheat ready for harvest. The fact of the harvest was never in question. People need Jesus. There was only a question of workers—people willing to reach those lost people. So the disciples were to pray that the Lord would send forth laborers. In other words, telling the good news about Jesus is for everyone, not just the professional clergy. If the work is to be done, it is to be done by ordinary Christians like you and me.

If we are to meet the pressing needs of our world, we must begin with prayer. How should you pray for missions? During your personal prayer time, include prayer for people you listed under Jerusalem who do not know Jesus. Pray that God would send people to your family and friends. Be prepared—God will often use *you* to reach those in your Jerusalem. Pray for yourself. Ask God to put people in your life daily that you can serve and/or share Jesus with. We must get out of the church and into the world where people are. We must mix and mingle with the lost, develop friendships with them, and out of those relationships share the good news of the kingdom of God. As a believer, you need to develop relationships with spiritually lost people so you can find avenues in which you can share your faith.

Consider this scenario. At 10:00 a.m. a van is coming to your church to take anyone who is willing to go to the mission field for the next six months. Will you get on the van?

Building the Kingdom

Missions help us to see that we can make a difference in the world! Trying to solve world hunger globally may seem insurmountable; however, working to get an orphanage in Mexico livable for 20 children is attainable!

Recently, a student ministry participated in building a new church in a small town in Colorado. The students went prepared to do Backyard Bible Clubs, puppets, music, and some work on the church itself. Upon arrival, it was discovered there were no children and the building schedule was three weeks behind! Instead of doing some singing, playing, and puppetry, students were taught how to install insulation and hang sheetrock. They came with shorts and T-shirts and ended up learning how to work with plastic taped to their arms and legs. What a stretching experience!

Some of the students weren't sure they had done anything that great that week. They wondered how a little work on a building could really make a difference. However, a few months later, the students received a card announcing the dedication of the building, now complete. Untold numbers of people will walk through the doors of that little church in Colorado and will meet the Jesus that each of those students served that summer. Those students will never know the effect of their week of labor on God's kingdom until they meet Jesus at His coming, but they get an awesome feeling knowing that people are in God's presence because they gave one summer week to help build a church.

Final Destination

If we are going to win our world for Jesus before His return, it will take all of us working together. Jesus said now is the time to "go!" (John 4:35-38) Although you may not be a career missionary, you can do your part in sharing God's love with others, even financially supporting and praying for those who go.

It will take all of us praying, giving, and going. Today's opportunities for missions are greater than ever before. Countries around the world need Christian teachers, medical professionals, agriculturists, scientists, contractors, and homemakers. Most of all, they need people who care so much about their eternity that those believers are willing to go.

Consider this scenario. At 10:00 a.m. a van is coming to your church to take anyone who is willing to go to the mission field for the next six months. Will you get on the van? What would happen if you got on the van? What would happen if you *didn't* get on the van?

Extra Credit

- Commit to pray for spiritually lost people in foreign countries. Develop a prayer calendar with the names of countries you want to pray for each day. Research facts and statistics about each country. You can find information about different people groups by going to *www.imb.org*.
- Read the personal testimonies of teens and adults who are sharing Jesus around the world. Look on the CD-ROM under "Missions and Ministry."
- Memorize Matthew 20:26-28.
- Talk to your pastor or youth minister about what you and/or your senior class can do locally in the areas of missions and service. Your pastor or youth minister may know of areas of service that you as students would be best qualified to accomplish.
- North American and international mission projects can be found at *www.namb.net* and *www.imb.org*. Go online and find the student mission project coordinator for your state. Contact the coordinator to find out about ways you can serve.

1. Testimony courtesy of the International Mission Board.

There are two freedoms—the false, where a man is free to do what he likes; the true, where a man is free to do what he ought. —Charles Kingsley

Chapter 12

FREE AT LAST

I n August 2004, Blake Hammontree entered the University of Oklahoma with a bright smile and a bright future. On September 30, his family mourned his death. The blood-alcohol content in his body measured 0.42, the equivalent of drinking 18 shots of 100-proof liquor in three hours. It was five times the legal limit.

That same fall, several alcohol-related deaths were reported in Colorado. Samantha Spady, a student at Colorado State, was found dead at a fraternity house after consuming as many as 30 drinks in 11 hours. At the University of Colorado, Lynn Gordon Bailey, Jr. (Gordie to his friends) was taken to the mountains near the university and told not to leave until he consumed several bottles of whiskey. He died as a result of this fraternity ritual. Twenty-year-old Amanda Morrison had a blood-alcohol level of 0.22 when she fell out of her dormitory window in Colorado Springs.

According to one report, there are an estimated 1,400 alcohol-related deaths each year among college students. Because the majority of these deaths are automobile-related, they generally go unnoticed.[1]

Some of what these students experienced was the misuse of freedom. Drinking may or may not seem like a temptation to you now, but it is one area you are likely to be exposed to when you graduate from high school. Knowing how to respond to temptation and handle your newfound freedom is a part of the essential gear you need to grasp before leaving home. During the next few years you'll not only learn more about yourself, but you'll also test some limits and for the first time experience the "real world." Does this freedom come with any restraints?

Choices and Consequences

Ask any high school senior what he is looking forward to after graduation, and greater freedom will be high on the list. Maybe you're looking forward to not having a parent check on your homework. Or you could be thrilled with the possibility of staying out all night without a curfew. Possibly you're just looking forward to exercising your independence—making choices on how you spend your time and money and who you hang out with. The freedom you're about to experience may seem unlimited, but you'll soon discover that the choices you make with that freedom can have lifelong consequences.

Maybe you've heard the phrase, "Your life is based on the choices you make." For the next four to six years of your life, this statement will never be truer. You'll be making many life-impacting decisions over the next few years. Some include:

- Choosing a work ethic that will either help or hinder your career path. This includes how you manage your time and how you respond to authorities.
- Setting moral boundaries. This can include your choices in regard to alcohol and drug abuse, physical intimacy, purity, and honesty.
- Choosing who you date and how serious the relationship will become. In the next six years you may contemplate marriage or make the choice to get married.
- Making career choices and whether you will or will not attend college. If you attend college, you'll be choosing a major emphasis of study and will even decide how many years you want to stay in school.
- Choosing to make your faith your own and not a faith handed down to you by your parents or a youth group. You will be seriously challenged to examine why you choose to follow Christ. It will be up to you to decide whether or not you are involved in church.

God-honoring Boundaries

Throughout your life, you have lived with certain boundaries. As an infant, you slept within the boundary of a crib. Why? So you wouldn't roll out and get hurt! As you grew, the boundaries expanded. You were given the freedom to explore the house and play in the backyard. But you still had the boundaries of walls in your house and a fence that kept you from running into the street. Over time, boundaries expanded even more. You were allowed to ride your bike in the neighborhood, walk to school, and sleep at a friend's house. In the last couple of years, you've even had the freedom to drive a car. You experienced more freedom because your parents were teaching you independence.

Did you still have boundaries during this time? Of course you did! The purpose of those boundaries was to protect you. If you follow the boundary of wearing a seat belt, you are much more protected from being injured in a car accident than if you fail to accept the boundary. You have the boundaries of speed limits, too. If you break the speed limit, you not only expose yourself to getting a ticket, but you expose yourself to the risk of being harmed.

The freedom you're about to experience may seem unlimited, but you'll soon discover that the choices you make with that freedom can have lifelong consequences.

Boundaries are God's idea—He established them from the very beginning of creation. In Genesis 2, God gave Adam and Eve boundaries in the garden of Eden. "And the Lord God commanded the man, 'You are free to eat from any tree of the garden, but you must not eat from the tree of the knowledge of good and evil, for on the day you eat from it, you will certainly die'" (Gen. 2:16-17). And what did Adam and Eve do? They struggled with the boundaries and ate the fruit from the tree of the knowledge of good and evil. Today, we are still suffering from their consequences!

The Israelites also struggled with freedom. Although they sought freedom from the Egyptians and God granted it to them, they had a history of turning their backs on God's authority. "In those days there was no king in Israel; everyone did whatever he wanted" (Judg. 17:6). The consequences? Idolatry, further captivity, and broken relationships with God.

Many people will argue that the Bible is a book full of rules to tell you no. You may even view your parents or other authority figures as roadblocks to freedom. However, God's Word is not His idea of restricting your fun or your independence. God created boundaries for your benefit, to help you now and in the future.

Up to this point in your life, your parents or guardians have set the boundaries. Galatians 4:2 says, "Instead, he is under guardians and stewards until the time set by his father." Why? Because your parents have experience—something you are lacking at this point in your life. The job of your parents is to help you balance freedom and responsibility. If they give you too little freedom, you will not gain experience and you'll be immature. But if you're given too much freedom, there is danger in being hurt. It's a fine line to walk, and now it's your turn to take that walk. You will experience greater freedom, but with that freedom comes increased responsibility.

So how do you prepare to handle your upcoming freedom? Will you accept your new freedoms with responsibility or will you forego God-honoring boundaries and suffer the consequences?

You will experience greater freedom, but with that freedom comes increased responsibility.

Experiencing God's Grace

The balance of freedom and responsibility was a key issue in the early church, especially in the region called Galatia. In response to their struggle, Paul wrote a letter to the people to try to help them. He wanted the believers to grasp the freedom God had given them through the grace of Christ. He wrote, "Christ has liberated us into freedom. Therefore stand firm and don't submit again to a yoke of slavery" (Gal. 5:1).

Paul was determined to get right to the heart of the problem. While many of the Jewish leaders were trying to convince new believers the laws of circumcision still applied, Paul urged the church to realize salvation comes from faith and faith alone. Paul taught that faith unlocks the door to the grace of God—the gift we cannot earn on our own.

So if we have freedom in Christ, do we have freedom from God's law? Can't we just do what we want because of God's unrelenting grace? Paul addressed this very issue in the Book of Romans. In chapter 6, he said, "What then? Should we sin because we are not under law but under grace? Absolutely not!" (Rom. 6:15). Paul knew the law was a standard no one could keep, but it helps define sin and leads us to recognize the need for living under God's authority and power.

Freedom's Choice: Live by the Flesh or Live by the Spirit

You have two choices in regard to how you are going to handle freedom after high school: you can choose to live a life that will follow your flesh, or you can live out your freedom guided by the Holy Spirit. When you accept Christ into your life, you receive the Holy Spirit. But you still have another nature—that's called the flesh. With each decision you make, you choose to follow the flesh (sinful desires) or the Spirit. It's a tough battle and one you'll face the rest of your life.

To understand this concept, think about two people on different diets. One person chooses a healthy diet of regular meals consisting of proteins, fruits, grains, and vegetables. The other person makes unhealthy choices—fast food, fried foods, and sweets. The person with the proper nutrition will reflect what she eats and be healthier. The one who makes poor choices will probably tend to be overweight and unhealthy.

Living by the flesh or the Spirit is somewhat like those two people. If you choose to feed the flesh by living a sinful life, you will be seen as someone who lives for himself. You will be spiritually unhealthy and will face consequences that cause pain to you and those around you. If you choose to feed your spirit by living on God's Word and following Him in obedience, your life will be led by the Holy Spirit. The result? You'll walk in the Spirit and in wisdom.

You have two choices in regard to how you are going to handle freedom after high school: you can choose to live a life that will follow your flesh, or you can live out your freedom guided by the Holy Spirit.

Living by the Flesh

To live by the flesh means to live for self. In Galatians 5:19-21, Paul gave a pretty good description of living in the flesh. He wrote, "Now the works of the flesh are obvious: sexual immorality, moral impurity, promiscuity, idolatry, sorcery, hatreds, strife, jealousy, outbursts of anger, selfish ambitions, dissensions, factions, envy, drunkenness, carousing, and anything similar." Did you notice the actions? They're all directed at self. At the heart of all of these is a selfish pursuit of some sort. Sexual immorality is self-centered. So are jealousy and envy. Carousing is too. A life in the flesh is a pursuit of selfish gain.

Living by the Holy Spirit

That list of sinful behaviors can be discouraging. But there is hope—found in pursuit of a life led by God's Spirit. Paul also wrote about what it's like to live by God's plan. He wrote, "But the fruit of the Spirit is love, joy, peace, patience, kindness, goodness, faith, gentleness, self-control. Against such things there is no law" (Gal. 5:22-23). A life lived by the power of God's Spirit will enable you to make good choices with your freedom. Listed below are some principles regarding exercising your freedom.

1. *Live out God's grace in serving others*. Take advantage of the opportunities you will have to serve others with your freedom. Galatians 5:13 says, "For you are called to freedom, brothers; only don't use this freedom as an opportunity for the flesh, but serve one another through love." Look for ways you can use your talents and time. Whether it's going on a mission trip or volunteering in your church, you can turn away from living in the flesh when you stop thinking about yourself and focus on others.

Just because you have more freedom when you graduate from high school doesn't mean you are free from all authority.

2. *Live differently from the world*. When you face temptations of the flesh— drinking, sexual promiscuity, or even watching an indecent movie—you can live by the Spirit by choosing to be different than the sinful world around you. While the world will tell you to live out your freedoms by experiencing every kind of pleasure you can, the consequences lead to slavery. In 2 Peter 2 there is a description of people who abuse their freedom. Eugene Peterson paraphrased it this way, "They promise these newcomers freedom, but they themselves are slaves of corruption, for if they're addicted to corruption—and they are—they're enslaved."[2] Take

a stand for what is right. People will respect your choices and may seek you out when they discover the emptiness of worldly pleasures.

3. *Live under the authorities God has placed over you.* Just because you have more freedom when you graduate from high school doesn't mean you are free from all authority. Adults still must respect government authorities, as well as authorities in their jobs, their churches, and ultimately, God's authority. Life without authority? That's called chaos. Just imagine what society would be without some of the laws that protect you. Or imagine a workplace where everyone is the president. God has placed authorities in our lives for a reason. Paul pointed out, "Everyone must submit to the governing authorities, for there is no authority except from God, and those that exist are instituted by God" (Rom. 13:1).

Reaping What You Sow

Have you ever heard the phrase, "You reap what you sow"? In other words, your actions carry consequences. If they were alive today, Blake Hammontree, Samantha Spady, and Lynn Gordon Bailey, Jr. would tell you that they paid dearly for their poor choices. They took seriously their freedom, but they didn't take into account the consequences of how they exercised their freedom.

Just as these students experienced the consequences of their actions, you must determine how you will exercise your freedom. As you make life-impacting decisions, ask yourself this important question: *Based on my past experiences, my present circumstances, and my future hopes and dreams, how will this decision affect my life?* The way you handle your freedoms will impact your journey into adulthood.

Extra Credit

- Memorize Galatians 2:20. If you seek to allow the Holy Spirit to live in you, your old life has to be crucified.
- Plan a high school graduation party that will honor God. Provide an alternative that will be fun but still avoids some of the traps of many other graduation parties.

1. Sources for alcohol information: Ken Raymond, "Friends recall OU student's bright outlook," *The Oklahoman*, 7 Nov. 2004; The Associated Press, "Ending the Hurt: Officials wonder what to do to stop alcohol-related deaths on campus," *The Telegraph* [online], [cited 29 Nov. 2004]. Available from Internet: *www.saulkvalley.com*; The Associated Press, "Colorado student dies after drinking," *The Oklahoman*, 7 Nov. 2004.
2. Eugene Peterson, *The Message* (Colorado Springs: NavPress Publishing Group, 2002).

True wisdom is to know what is best worth knowing, and to do what is best worth doing.
—Laurence Humphrey

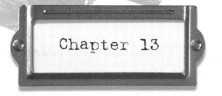

Chapter 13

GET OFF
THE FENCE

105

H ave you ever considered how many decisions you will make in the next five years? College or career? Pre-med or pre-law? Dorm or apartment? Army or Air Force? Work at the grocery store or the factory? Greek or independent? Single or married? Paper or plastic? Someone once said that the majority of life-changing decisions are made between the ages of 18 and 25. There should be a preparation period, a class or course you could take to get ready to make these weighty and complicated decisions. Unfortunately, you can't take a prep course to study up on making decisions, so the next seven years will be an adventure in decision making.

Consider some of the decisions you have made this year. What principles did you use to make those decisions? Why did you choose to date that person? Why did you play baseball? Why did you drink at that party? Why did you sign an abstinence pledge card? Why did you wear that prom dress? Some decisions you made were based on careful, analytical thought. Other were based on no thought whatsoever. In the next few years, the decisions you make could be much more than embarrassing; they could carry far-reaching consequences. As you prepare for the next chapter in your life, make certain that you have a set of principles that will guide your decision making.

The Wealthy Boys

Once upon a time (don't worry, this isn't a fairy tale), there were two men with pockets full of cash. One was young and powerful, the other short and hated. They had two things common—wealth and a sense of unfulfill-ment.

You may have heard about the rich, young ruler. His story is found in Luke 18:18-23. He was evidently a man who had some type of political position among his people. Although he probably could have been named "bachelor of the month," he had one problem—a nagging sense that there was "something more." He just wasn't content within himself.

You've also heard about the other man, Zacchaeus. (Luke 19:1-10) He was older, shorter, and utterly despised by everyone he knew. He worked for the Roman government collecting taxes from his own people to give the money to the occupying Roman authority. Whatever he could collect above the minimum tax he could keep for himself. No one swooned as he walked by; in fact, he probably had to duck as he walked to avoid being hit by flying objects thrown by his neighbors. Like the rich young ruler, he had pockets full of cash and one problem—he was not comfortable within himself.

Our decisions are based on what we value.

Within a matter of a few days, both men would encounter Jesus as He made His way toward Jerusalem for the last time. Both men had heard of the miracle worker, and both wanted to see Him face-to-face. What each did not know was that his encounter with Jesus would demand a reckoning of his priorities—what he worshiped. It is this encounter with Jesus in our own lives that illuminates the heart of our decision making. Why? Because our decisions are based on what we value.

The Saddest Decision

Have you ever met a person who seems to have everything? The rich, young ruler must have appeared this way to his peers—in control, wealthy, need-ing nothing. To his credit, he approached Jesus and fell to his knees. He wanted to know what he needed to do to inherit "eternal life." This wasn't an unusual question. The Jewish rabbis often discussed this question and disagreed about the answer. Therefore, it was not strange for this man to ask Jesus, the Rabbi, His opinion on inheriting eternal life.

In answering the question, Jesus lured him in by giving him the answer he wanted; then Jesus gave him the one answer he could not handle. First, Jesus talked about the commandments that deal with interpersonal relationships. (See Ex. 20:12-16.) When the man said he'd kept those laws faithfully, Jesus then told the ruler to sell all his possessions, give to the poor and needy, walk away from all he possessed, and follow Him. (See Luke 18:22.) At this point, the conversation ended—the young man "went away grieving" (Matt. 19:22). Why? Because the rich, young ruler's life was directed by his many possessions. He couldn't give those up to follow Jesus. He had placed so much value in his possessions on this earth, so his ability to make good decisions was hampered; he chose to make money his god instead of the Savior.

The Little Tax Collector That Did

To fully appreciate this story, you need to get a mental image of our friend Zacchaeus. He was definitely short and definitely hated. He probably had a nice home in town, but he had no joy. One day he heard that Jesus, the miracle-working prophet, was in town. Zacchaeus might have gained a special interest in this Jesus, because a former fellow tax collector named Matthew had become one His followers.

As the noise of the crowds filled the city of Jericho, Zacchaeus headed out to find a place where he could get a glimpse of Jesus, the lover of tax collectors. When he couldn't find a place to see over the crowds lining the streets, this dignified symbol of Roman authority did what any wealthy man would do—he climbed a tree!

As Jesus walked along the street, He stopped—seeing a grown man in expensive clothes sitting in a tree is reason to stop. Not only did Jesus stop, but He invited Himself to Zacchaeus's house for dinner—a scandalous act for a God-fearing Jew. And before dinner was finished, more scandal erupted. Zacchaeus, the greedy, money-hungry tax collector, pledged to give half of his possessions to the poor and to give back four times over anything he had overcharged people for their taxes.

What could have led to this type of decision making? Simple. He saw more value in Jesus than in his money. While the rich, young ruler was a slave to his money and could not bear to lose his fortune no matter the consequences, Zacchaeus could not wait to give up the possessions he had. Why? Because Jesus simply told Zacchaeus what he had been dying to hear: life is much more than your possessions. That resulted in some life-altering decisions in Zacchaeus's life.

Values and Decisions

Just like Zacchaeus and the rich, young ruler, we all make decisions based upon what we value. If you go to a party to hang out with the popular crowd even though you know it'll hurt your reputation, then your popularity is more important to you than your character. If you choose to go to college because you hope to get a better job later, then education is important to you. Most often, we base our decisions on what we value.

Over the next few years, you'll be faced with countless decisions. Some will carry heavy consequences. Others will be minor. Maybe you will have to choose whether you go to a movie with your friends or study for a final exam. If your social time with friends is of value, then you will probably choose the movie. If your academics are important, then you will stay and study. Or maybe you'll choose both (you *can* study and still have fun). Perhaps you will decide to get married. If your spiritual maturity is important to you, then you will date a person (hopefully!) whose faith is important as well. The question you need to ask yourself before you have to make decisions is, *What has value, worth, and importance in my life?*

Where Are You Leaning?

One of the most common Scriptures you're probably hearing as a graduating senior is found in the Book of Proverbs: "Trust in the LORD with all your heart, and do not rely on your own understanding; think about Him in all your ways, and He will guide you on the right paths" (Prov. 3:5-6). These verses actually contain three important truths to rely on when making a decision.

1. *Trust God with all your heart.* Why can you trust God with all your heart? Because God is completely trustworthy. God always acts in keeping with His character, and His character is good. He doesn't change like the shadows. (See Jas. 1:17.) You can ask God to show you the right decision to make, but you must trust His response, even if it doesn't seem the easiest or the most beneficial.
2. *Don't rely on your own understanding of a situation.* God knows

everything—you don't. Rely on His perfect wisdom. Imagine you are a pilot sitting in a cockpit and you are totally blinded by a cloud or fog. The only thing on which you can rely is your instruments. After a while, you begin to panic because what you are feeling is not consistent with what the instruments are showing you. Do you rely on the instruments or on your feelings? Of course, you rely on the instruments because they are consistent. The same applies to your decisions. God is consistent and wise. What do you do when your friends are headed to the club for drinks? Your date is moving too fast? Your boss wants you to lie or steal? If your standards are based on feelings in the moment, you may wake up facing some serious consequences. Relying on your limited decision-making resources is like ignoring the instruments of the plane.

With God as the One on whom we rely, we risk nothing because it is in His best interest to give us wise counsel.

3. *Think about God when you're making a decision.* The *New International Version* reads, "In all your ways acknowledge Him" (Prov. 3:6). Loosely interpreted, to acknowledge God is to place His name on all we do and say. Military personnel acknowledge their country with the flag on their uniforms, and fans at a sporting event acknowledge their loyalty by wearing gear with the team name or mascot. To acknowledge means to choose your actions according to those things that would honor God's name. Some choices you make would not honor God. Avoid them. There is no better way to clear out your selfish motives and your rationalizations than to demand that every decision carry the approval of God.

Practical Points

OK. So you're trusting God with all your heart. You're leaning on His wisdom and understanding. And you're seeking to honor Him. You're seeking Him and His wisdom to guide you. But you still have a decision to make. What are some practical tips for making decisions? What questions should you ask yourself before you proceed with a course of action? Use the following questions to help you determine a course of action.

1. *Have I sought godly advice?* When you're facing a tough decision, it's a good idea to seek out the wisdom of godly men and women. Notice the word *godly*. That's the key. Don't go to your frat buddies to tell them about your struggle with going partying. They won't give you sound advice. If you know that you won't like the answer that a godly person would give you, then you've got your answer.

When in doubt, don't. You'll save yourself a lot of grief.

2. *How will this affect important relationships?* If your boyfriend is pressuring you to spend your free time only with him, your relationship with others will be drastically affected in a negative way. If your boss is offering you overtime at the expense of your Bible study group, then maybe you shouldn't work so many hours. If a choice would cause you to abandon relationships that God has brought into your life, then it's probably not a good choice.
3. *Is this activity the best use of my time and energy?* You'll have the opportunity to join clubs, get involved in service organizations, and even pick up new hobbies. Contrary to popular belief among young adults, you can't do everything. You must choose the activities, sports, classes, relationships, and hobbies that are most important. Make choices based on what is the best use of your time, energy, gifts, and talents.
4. *Have I taken the time to think this through or am I feeling pressured to decide immediately?* Remember, haste makes mistakes. If you make a decision when you feel rushed or pressured by outside influences, you're more likely to make a mistake. Take time to step back, evaluate the pros and cons of the decision, and take your time. And when in doubt, don't. You'll save yourself a lot of grief.

Equal Options

Most Christians get stuck in the decision-making process when they have two equally worthy options and they do not know which godly choice to make. What do you do when God seems to be saying yes to both of your options? One year at youth camp, the camp pastor told us that he could tell us what God's will was for our lives. I was excited because I was struggling with some decisions and I needed clear direction. That night the pastor told me that God's will for my life was first, to love God, and second, to love others. He went on to say that if I faced any decision in which both options fulfill those two standards, then I could just pick one and go with it. Could it really be that simple? Yes. If you are struggling with a decision, talk to God about it. He may be allowing you to choose one of several options, each of which would bring honor to Him and is in keeping with Scripture. If God really wants you to choose one over the other and you are praying about it, do you think He will sit quietly while you choose something else? Wouldn't happen! God will make Himself clear.

God is a good God and wants to guide you into the very best for your life if you're willing to go where He leads.

Whether you choose tater tots or fries, blue jeans or shorts, early childhood education or biochemical engineering, or even paper or plastic, the decision you make will come down to what is of value to you. The key is properly setting your estimation of value on the right things in your life. Make your decisions by trusting God, leaning on Him for His wisdom, and seeking to honor Him with your actions. Ask some tough questions and be willing to act on the answers. Remember, God is a good God and wants to guide you into the very best for your life if you're willing to go where He leads.

Extra Credit
- Think about some decisions you need to make this week. Use the principles and questions in this book to help you make wise decisions.
- Spend time reflecting on some poor decisions you have made during your high school years. Spend some time with God, asking Him for His forgiveness where necessary. Also thank Him for being a God who can turn even your mistakes into things that honor Him.

What Are You chasing?

The Pursuit

Milt Hughes